THE TOTAL LATIN GUITARIST

>> A Fun and Comprehensive Overview of Latin Guitar Playing

DOUG MUNRO

Alfred, the leader in educational publishing,

and the National Guitar Workshop,

one of America's finest guitar schools, have joined

forces to bring you the best, most progressive

educational tools possible. We hope you will enjoy

this book and encourage you to look for

other fine products from Alfred and the

National Guitar Workshop.

ISBN-10: 0-7390-6950-0 (Book & CD)
ISBN-13: 978-0-7390-6950-9 (Book & CD)

This book was acquired, edited, and produced
by Workshop Arts, Inc., the publishing arm of
the National Guitar Workshop.
Nathaniel Gunod, acquisitions, managing editor
Burgess Speed, acquisitions, senior editor
Timothy Phelps, interior design
Ante Gelo, music typesetter
CD recorded and mastered by Collin Tilton at Bar None Studio, Northford, CT
Doug Munro (guitar), Michael Goetz (bass), Tony Garcia (percussion)

Cover photograph by Jim Frank
Guitar on cover courtesy Aria Guitars and Dana B. Goods

Table of Contents

About the Author

Doug Munro is a critically acclaimed New York jazz guitarist. Since 1987, he has released 11 albums as a bandleader and has appeared on over 50 recordings as a sideman, producer, and arranger, working with a diverse array of artists including Dr. John, Michael Brecker, and Dr. Lonnie Smith. Doug has over 75 published compositions and over 300 recorded arrangements by the finest players on the scene today.

Doug has received two Grammy nominations and two NAIRD awards. Amazon.com picked *Boogaloo to Beck*, which Doug performed on, arranged, and co-produced, as one of its Top Ten Jazz CDs of 2003. Doug also did orchestration work on the Oscar-winning 1997 documentary *When We Were Kings*. Doug continues to actively perform with around 100 live dates per year.

As an educator, Doug created and was Director of the Jazz Studies Program at The Conservatory of Music at Purchase College from 1993–2002. He continues to teach there as Director Emeritus. This esteemed jazz program boasts a faculty that includes John Abercrombie, Todd Coolman, Jon Faddis, Eric Alexander, John Riley, and many other top jazz performers.

Doug has written three books on jazz improvisation for Alfred Music Publishing:

- *Swing to Bebop* (Alfred 00-0388B) (Winner of The Music and Sound Retailers' Instructional Book of the Year Award in 2000)
- *Bebop and Beyond* (Alfred 00-0609B)
- *Organ Trio Blues* (Alfred 00-0758B)

Additional information is available at Doug's website: www.dougmunro.com

PHOTO BY JIM FRANK

Acknowledgements

There are many people who helped make this book possible. I would first like to thank Aaron Stang, my long-time editor and friend, from back in the Warner Brothers days. After Alfred Music Publishing merged with Warner, it was Aaron who put me in touch with the people at Workshop Arts, who co-publish many instructional music books with Alfred. Thanks to Jason Shadrick for introducing me to everyone at Workshop Arts; he has always been very generous with his time and contacts, and his help and friendship has been invaluable to completing this project. Next up is Burgess Speed, my new editor; working with Burgess has been great, he has a solid view of the "big picture" but never loses sight of the small details involved in writing a meaningful book. I look forward to, hopefully, doing many more projects together. Thanks also to Gil Parris, a longtime friend and guitarist. His generosity in helping me with this, and pretty much every project I've ever done, is greatly appreciated. Lastly, I would like to thank the good Lord for his love and guidance and my wife, Kathleen, and my sons, Eugene and John, for their love and support.

Introduction

This book is intended for the intermediate to advanced guitarist who has an interest in exploring Latin guitar styles. To get the most out of this book, you should have a firm grasp on playing technique and theory, including scale theory, chord theory, and diatonic harmony. You should also be able to read standard music notation or tablature (TAB). For a refresher on some of these topics, refer to the Appendix on page 126.

The Total Latin Guitarist is a sampler of 23 different Latin music styles from six different countries. For every famous person mentioned in this book, there are many more that are not mentioned. In doing the research for this book, I found many contrasting explanations and points of view on musical and historical information. This book only includes material that musicians and historians are in general agreement about.

Many of the common questions asked by musicians studying Latin music are addressed in these pages. Concepts like the clave and specific rhythmic patterns are explained and demonstrated. All of the examples are hands-on, practical solutions for creating the distinctive sounds of each style.

The Total Latin Guitarist, while not a history book, provides some background on each style of music played. Gaining a historical perspective on the music helps in interpreting and understanding the particular harmonic and rhythmic patterns intrinsic to each style.

Every recording listed in this book is still available (at least at the time of this publishing). It is vital that you listen to the music that you study in this book. There are subtleties that can only be learned through immersing yourself in the music.

Be sure to memorize the musical examples and play along with the recorded tracks on the CD.

As you master the information in this book, it is vital that you go out and play it. Get together with like-minded musicians and play in these styles. There is a whole other education you get from playing and sharing this music with others. Most of all, it is so much fun to feel the groove and be a part of making this unique and exciting music.

0

Track 1

A compact disc is available with this book. Using the disc will help make learning more enjoyable and the information more meaningful. Listening to the CD will help you correctly interpret the rhythms and feel of each example. The symbol to the left appears next to each song or example that is performed on the CD. Example numbers are above the symbol. The track number below each symbol corresponds directly to the song or example you want to hear. Track 1 will help you tune your guitar to this CD.

Chapter 1: Latin Accompaniment Techniques

While the various styles and sub-styles covered in this book seem quite diverse, there are certain general accompaniment techniques that apply to them all.

There are generally two styles of guitar accompaniment in this book:

1. The style used when there is *no* bass instrument present.

2. The style used when there *is* a bass instrument present.

Some of the styles covered in this book do not feature guitar in the original instrumentation. In these cases, the guitar part is the result of combining and adapting the harmonic and rhythmic elements of non-guitar instruments.

Accompaniment Styles Without a Bass Instrument

Throughout this book, you will see numerous examples of accompaniment parts that utilize an alternating single-note bass line and chord pattern. The bass line typically alternates between the root and 5th of the chord. In these cases, the guitarist is fulfilling the requirement of the bass part in the absence of a bass instrument.

The accompaniment styles can be approached in any one of the following three ways:

1. With a traditional, classical fingerstyle approach. Play the bass line with the thumb, and the chords with the fingers.

2. With a hybrid pick-and-finger approach, with the pick playing the bass notes, and the 2nd, 3rd, and 4th fingers of the right-hand playing the chords

3. With a pick.

Each type of right-hand approach yields a different sound and presents certain physical challenges.

Following are the three types of right-hand approaches with an alternating bass line.

Fingerstyle Approach

The first example is to be played fingerstyle using classical right-hand fingering. The thumb is indicated with *p* (the Spanish word for "thumb" is *pulgar*), *i* is for index, *m* is for middle, and *a* is for ring (the Spanish word for "ring" is *anillo*).

Note: Even though the following examples are written in $\frac{4}{4}$ for easier reading, they should be played with a cut time feel. (For more about this, see page 14.)

Right-Hand Fingers

p	=	thumb
i	=	index
m	=	middle
a	=	ring

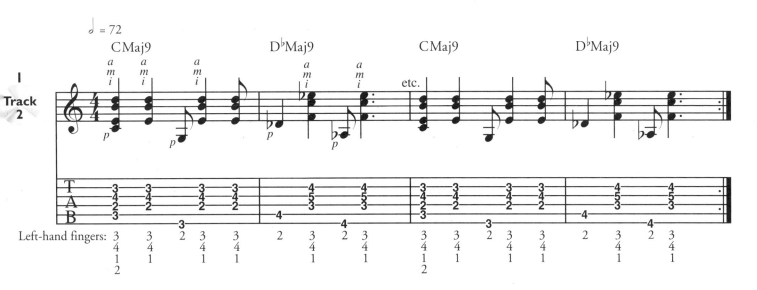

Hybrid-Picking Approach

The next example utilizes the hybrid pick-and-finger approach. The letters *pi* represent the thumb and index finger used to hold the pick. The letters *m* and *a* still represent the middle and ring fingers. The letter *c* represents the pinky (*chiquito* in Spanish).

Right-Hand Fingers

pi	=	pick
c	=	pinky

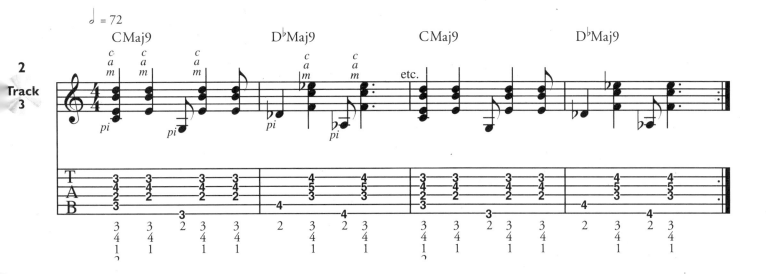

Pick-Style Approach

The final accompaniment style involves using just the pick and no fingers. This is typical of the "Gypsy Jazz"–style players.

■ = Downstroke of pick

Accompaniment Styles with a Bass Instrument

Once you add a bass player to the mix, it frees the guitarist from the role of playing the bass notes. However, there is nothing wrong with continuing to play the bass notes, but you do need to be "on the same page" with the bassist to avoid conflicting bass lines.

Following, we will look at the same bossa nova pattern played with the three right-hand approaches. Now, however, there will be no alternating bass figure, as this would be played by the bass player.

Fingerstyle Approach

The first example is to be played fingerstyle with classical right-hand fingering.

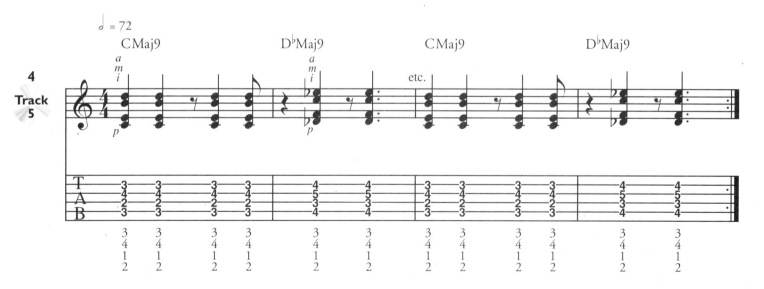

Hybrid-Picking Approach

The next example utilizes the hybrid pick-and-finger approach.

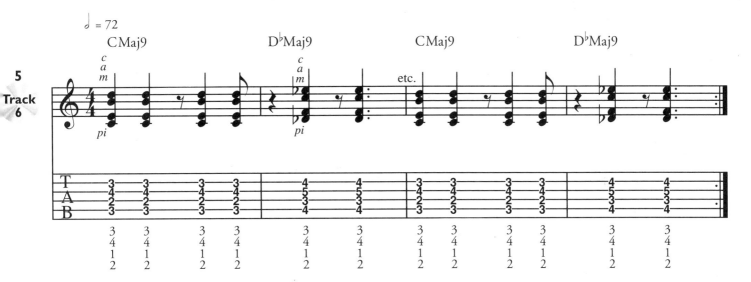

Pick-Style Approach

Now, we will use just the pick.

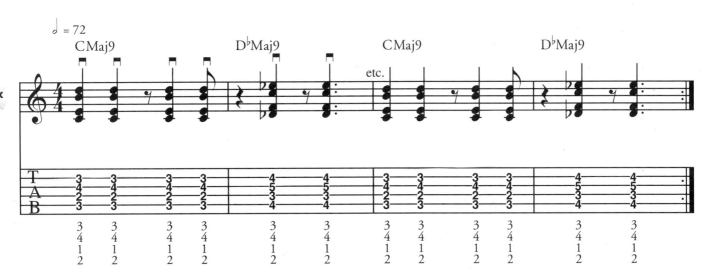

Chapter 2: Latin Soloing Techniques

At the end of each musical style covered in this book, there is an example of a single-line improvisation in that style. While each style has its own unique characteristics, there are general approaches to improvising that apply to all the styles in this book.

The importance of listening to and transcribing the various styles in this book cannot be emphasized enough. Also, remember that there are no "absolutes" in music theory. There is always an exception to every rule. The music came first, the theory is just an explanation of what has been played.

With that being said, following are some general guidelines for improvising over the musical styles presented in this book.

Many Latin styles are based on traditional European harmony and African rhythm. The improvisation used is based on these two ingredients. Many players focus on the harmonic portion, while neglecting the rhythmic portion. However, both are equally important.

To improvise successfully you need to have a "basket" of soloing concepts, transcribed riffs, motifs, etc. to draw from. Scales, modes, and arpeggios are often mistaken for these basket items; they are not. Scales, modes, and arpeggios are the tools that are used to create the items in your basket.

Soloing Based on a Scale or Mode

Below is a C Major scale. It is an important tool used to make music.

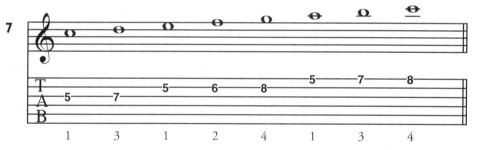

Below is a Latin-style riff taken from the notes of the C Major scale. This riff has all the ingredients of a good solo statement:

1. It fits over the harmony of the CMaj7 chord.
2. It leaps intervals within the measures and moves *stepwise* (movements in half steps or whole steps) across the barlines.
3. It utilizes Latin rhythms, which are highly *syncopated*. (Syncopation is what occurs when emphasis is placed on parts of the beat, or measure, that are not usually emphasized.)

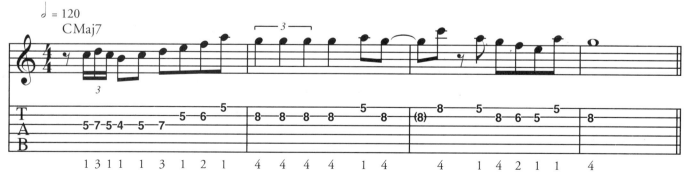

This riff can go in my "basket." I can use it on any C major tonality.

Here is the same riff over a *diatonic* chord progression in C Major. (Diatonic just means "within the key.")

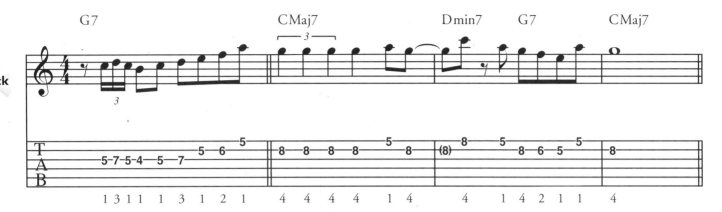

Soloing Based on an Arpeggio

The term *arpeggio* refers to the notes of a chord played individually, rather than simultaneously. Below is a CMaj9 arpeggio, which consists of scale degrees 1–3–5–7–9.

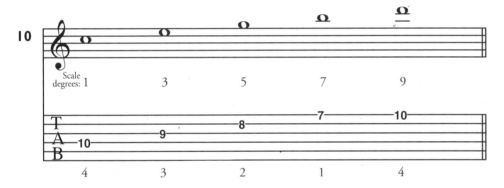

The following example is a Latin-style riff taken from the notes of the CMaj9 arpeggio. This riff also possesses ingredients for a good solo statement:

1. It fits over the harmony of the CMaj9 chord.

2. It utilizes syncopated Latin rhythms.

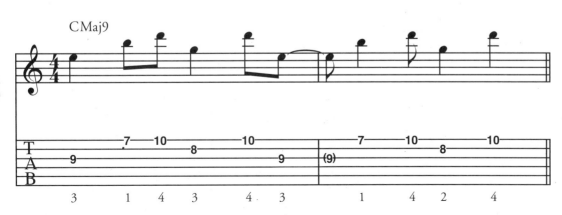

Before each summary solo in this book, all the scales, modes, and arpeggios used in that solo will be mentioned. You should learn each solo exactly as it is written, and then combine that info with the listed tools (scales, modes, and arpeggios) to create your own lines, phrases, and riffs.

Voice Leading

Voice leading is the technique used to connect two different scales, modes, arpeggios, or chords. Smooth voice leading involves connecting the above by no more than a whole step. Good voice leading creates better flowing single lines and better chord connections.

Next, we will look at two concepts you can use to improve your single-note voice leading.

Guide Tones

In general, *guide tones* are the 3rd and 7th note of the scale, mode, arpeggio, or chord that you are on. When the harmony moves in cycle (the *cycle of descending 5ths,* see page 127), you can connect the 7th of the chord you are on to the 3rd of the chord you are going to. This creates a smoother transition between chords.

Below is an example of guide tone connections in a solo phrase over a ii–V–I chord progression in C Major (for Roman numerals and Diatonic Harmony, see page 127). These three chords are moving in cycle (G is a 5th below D, and C is a 5th below G). Notice that the 7th (C) of Dmin7 leads to the 3rd (B) of G7. Likewise, the 7th (F) of G7 leads to the 3rd (E) of CMaj7.

12 Track 11

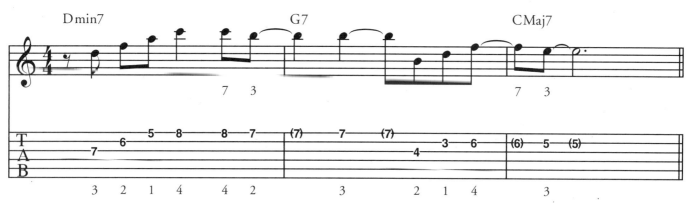

Notice in the previous example the use of another common voice-leading technique that we have already mentioned: *step across, leap within*. This just means that whenever you are on a particular chord, scale, or mode, you can use leaping intervals within the measures, but you should move stepwise across the barline, or chord change.

Chord Connections

Try to connect all the notes in your chord by no more than a whole step. This will yield better-sounding chord progressions.

Following is the chord accompaniment to Example 12, using smooth chord connections.

13
Track 12

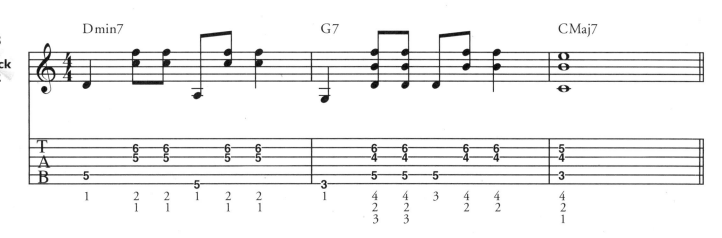

In the example above, you can see that the bass notes are playing the root and 5th of each chord, while the upper notes are connecting by whole step or half step.

For an in-depth look at guitar harmony, you may refer to the following books:

  Swing to Bebop (Alfred 00-0388B)

  Bebop and Beyond (Alfred 00-0609B)

  Organ Trio Blues (Alfred 00-0758B)

Chapter 3: Clave

Son Clave

Son is a style of Afro-Cuban music that originated in the second half of the 19th century in the province of Oriente in Cuba (see page 18). Arsenio Rodríguez is credited with creating the modern Afro-Cuban sound. Arsenio played the *tres,* a three-course, six-stringed, guitar-like instrument (see illustration below). The tres is tuned G–C–E, with the two strings in each course tuned in unison. The son *clave,* a rhythmic figure that is the foundation of many Latin musical styles, is most associated with dance music. *Claves* also refer to the instruments that play this rhythm. They consist of two sticks that produce a distinct sound when struck together (see illustration below). The son clave rhythm is two bars long, and the order of these two bars may be reversed, depending on the music's melody.

3-2 Son Clave

Following is the *3-2 son clave,* which is sometimes referred to as the *forward clave.* It has three accents in the first measure and two in the second.

Guitar.   *Tres.*

There is no time signature in the example above in order to show you that there are two ways to think about the clave.

The easiest way to count the clave is in $\frac{4}{4}$ time:

1, 2-**&**, 3, **4**, 1, **2**, **3**, 4

The easiest way to feel the clave is in $\frac{2}{2}$, or *cut time,* where there are two beats in each measure and the half note receives one beat:

1-E-&-**A**, 2-**&**, 1-**&**, **2**

2-3 Son Clave

The *2-3 son clave* is sometimes referred to as the *reverse clave.* It has two accents in the first measure and three in the second.

Again, the easiest way to count the clave is in $\frac{4}{4}$ time:

1, **2**, **3**, 4, **1**, 2-**&**, 3, **4**

The easiest way to feel the clave is in $\frac{2}{2}$ time:

1-**&**, **2**, **1**-E-&-**A**, 2-**&**

Claves.

Rumba Clave

As the son style of music progressed and became popular, the *rumba* style grew in popularity. The *rumba clave* and style is more associated with folkloric rhythms which have more of a $\frac{6}{8}$ feel. Rumba comes from the word *rumbear,* which literally means "going to parties, dancing, and having a good time." The rumba is strongly connected to drumming, singing, and dancing.

Below are two rumba claves.

3-2 Rumba Clave

The *3-2 rumba clave* is distinguished by the *anticipation* of the last note in the first measure. It anticipates, or creates a strong movement towards, the *downbeat* (beat 1) of the second measure.

The best way to count the 3-2 rumba clave is in $\frac{4}{4}$ time:

1, 2-**&**, 3, 4-**&**, 1, **2**, **3**, 4

The best way to feel the clave is in $\frac{2}{2}$ time:

1-E-&-**A**, 2-E-&-**A**, 1-**&**, **2**

2-3 Rumba Clave

In the *2-3 rumba clave,* the measures are reversed, and the anticipation is placed on the last beat of the second measure.

Count this clave in $\frac{4}{4}$ time:

1, **2**, **3**, 4, **1**, 2-**&**, 3, 4-**&**

Feel this clave in $\frac{2}{2}$ time:

1-**&**, **2**, 1-E-&-**A**, 2-E-&-**A**

Practice Tip

Take your metronome and set it to 100bpm (100 beats per minute). Clap the rhythms with the $\frac{4}{4}$ count. Practice this until you can clap the rhythm without counting. Now, set the metronome to 60bpm. Clap the rhythm with the $\frac{2}{2}$, or cut time, feel. Once you have this internalized, try clapping the various claves at different tempos.

Bossa Clave

There is debate on whether there truly are claves outside of Afro-Cuban music. However, through playing and listening to Brazilian music, one can discern a clave that is present in some styles, especially bossa nova. Here, the clave is used differently than in Afro-Cuban music. The pattern is usually played by the drummer using the *cross-stick* technique on the snare drum. (This technique involves the hitting of the rim in a special way that is meant to simulate the sound of the claves.)

The *bossa clave* is not based on the melody. In theory, it can be played forward or reverse, though the forward pattern (3-2) is the standard.

3-2 Bossa Clave

In the *3-2 bossa clave,* notice that the accent in the second measure is shifted from the "3" to the "& of 3."

18
Track
17

The bossa nova is played in $\frac{4}{4}$ time.

Here is how you would count the 3-2 bossa clave:

1, 2-**&**, 3, **4**, 1, **2**, 3-**&**, 4

2-3 Bossa Clave

The measures are simply reversed in the *2-3 bossa clave.*

19
Track
18

Count the 2-3 bossa clave in the following way:

1, **2**, 3-**&**, 4, **1**, 2-**&**, 3, **4**

It is essential that you listen to musical examples of son, rumba, and bossa claves. For examples of these different rhythmic styles, listen to recordings of the artists listed to the right.

> ## Suggested Listening
>
> Son clave—Arsenio Rodríguez
> Compay Segundo
>
> Rumba clave—Israel "Cachao" López
> Orquesta Aragón
>
> Bossa clave—João Gilberto
> Antônio Carlos Jobim

Chapter 4: Montuno/Guajeo

The *montuno,* or *guajeo,* is a two-bar pattern that follows the clave. There is an interesting relationship between the montuno and the guajeo. Many guitarists adapt piano montunos to the guitar. We will be doing that many times throughout this book. It should be pointed out, however, that the style called "guajeo" was first developed on the tres and was later adapted by piano players and called "montuno."

Remember that the clave follows the melody. The busier, or more syncopated, side of the melody is usually the "3" side of the clave. The montuno/guajeo most often consists of the notes of chords played as arpeggios, with special detail given to the chord connections using the guide tones (3rds and 7ths) of each chord.

Following is a typical guajeo pattern in the Arsenio Rodríguez style. Note that this pattern follows the 2-3 clave. Use the fingerstyle approach for this one.

On the CD, you will hear two count-off clicks, then the clave, then the example. Remember, these examples are written in $\frac{4}{4}$ time for easier reading, but should be played with a "2" feel, or cut time.

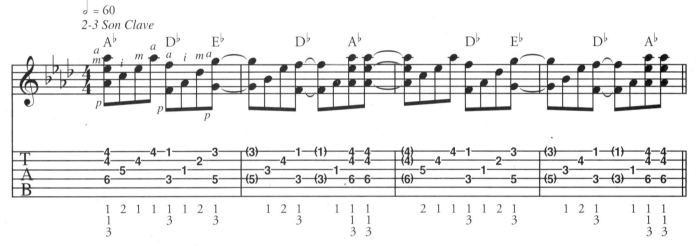

Below is a typical montuno in the style of Eddie Palmieri. Eddie Palmieri is a great Puerto Rican-born piano player who won the first-ever Grammy Award for Best Latin Recording. For this one, you could use a pick, play it fingerstyle, or even use the hybrid-picking technique.

Chapter 5: Afro-Cuban

CUBA

Havana

Cuban music has its roots in Europe, Africa, and America. The booming sugar trade that began at the turn of the 19th century transformed Cuba into a plantation society, and the demand for African slaves, who had been introduced into Cuba from Spain in the early part of the 16th century, greatly increased. The slave trade with the West African coast exploded, with around 400,000 Africans brought to Cuba from 1835–1864. The slave trade was abolished in 1886.

The two most influential strains of Cuban popular music can be roughly categorized into two groups: the *danzón* and the son.

The danzón style resulted from the blending of two cultures. The Spanish colonists brought religious and secular music to Cuba, and the Spanish dance music was enjoyed by all the social strata. The two converging cultures of the working-class Spanish and African peoples developed into the danzón from the European-based *contradanza*.

A good group to check out is Orquesta la Moderna Tradición, since they specialize in the traditional danzón. It is thought that the clave, as it is used in Afro-Cuban music, developed from the *cinquillo*. The cinquillo is the central pattern played on the timbales (see illustration below). The "3" part of the claves, it is believed, came from the first bar of this pattern. Check out the cinquillo pattern to the left.

Timbales.

The Cinquillo Pattern

Staccato. Sharp, detached.

22

Son

The music style son originated in eastern Cuba in the Oriente province, and it laid the foundation for the international genre called *salsa*. The early son was a vocal music accompanied by tres, guitar, and maracas (see illustration below). By the 1920s, this instrumentation was augmented with the addition of brass instruments. This was an American influence. Much of the early jazz in New Orleans was influenced by the military bands of the era. The *son montuno*, a type of son, increased the number of musicians by adding a three-trumpet horn section, a piano, and a conga drum (see illustration below and to the right). The parallels to the early American big band are interesting.

Arsenio Rodríguez was a major contributor to this music. Blinded from a kick to the head by a horse, he was known as *El Ciego Maravilloso* ("The Marvellous Blind Man"). Arsenio played the tres. He also came to America to find a cure for his blindness. That didn't work out but his trip to the states put him in touch with the jazz scene, especially Dizzy Gillespie and Tito Puente. Arsenio eventually migrated to the United States in 1952. Check out the recording *The Music of Cuba, Arsenio Rodríguez, Vol. 1*.

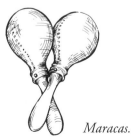

Maracas.

Conga.

Salsa

Salsa refers to a particular style of Afro-Cuban music developed in the 1960s and '70s by Puerto Rican and Cuban immigrants in the New York area. Its roots are in the Cuban son and mambo (see page 36). Salsa is essentially a dance music. The word *salsa* literally means "sauce." Salsa, which also has a strong Puerto Rican influence, is the broadest term for all Latin-based styles of music. The exact scope of the music is subject to some debate. To the right is a list of salsa artists and recordings to check out.

Suggested Listening

Tito Puente—*Dance Mania* (Legacy Edition, Sony Music Entertainment, 2009)

Ray Barretto—*The Essential Ray Barretto: A Man and His Music* (Emusica Records, 2007)

Eddie Palmieri—*The Best of Eddie Pamieri* (Charly Records, 2006)

Salsa Accompaniment

Below is an example of a salsa montuno. Remember, salsa is a very general term used to describe Afro-Cuban music. It is usually associated with up-tempo dance. This example is in an arpeggio style with the notes of the harmony played one at a time. This example is easiest when played with the fingerstyle approach.

The example above was transcribed from a piano montuno. Notice how each new chord starts with octaves.

Note: Bass lines have been included in all the musical examples in this book so you can see and hear how the guitar and bass parts work together (along with the percussion) to create the different feels. Remember to listen to the CD to hear the examples performed by a full band.

This next montuno is a ii–V–I chord progression in A♭ Major (see Diatonic Harmony, page 127). The bass notes descend by half step or whole step, while the top of each chord stays stationary.

24
Track
22

You can see that there is more chord action going on in this example. You can tell the "2" side of the clave by the measure that is less syncopated.

Salsa Solo

The example on the next page features two salsa montunos in the same style as the two we just looked at. In addition, there is a single-note improvisation over the top of them.

Notice in the first half of this example that the improvisation line never plays on beat 1. This helps to further syncopate and propel the line forward.

The line is very diatonic and sticks mostly to the B♭ Major scale. In the second half of the example, we switch to the G Harmonic Minor scale (a harmonic minor scale is made up of scale degrees 1–2–♭3–4–5–♭6–7). Here, the leading tone, the 7 (F♯), is emphasized to really make you feel the G Minor tonality. This line may give you some ideas if you are called on to improvise in this style. It is suggested that you listen to some trumpet players, as well as guitar players, because the trumpet is one of the primary improvisational instruments in this style of music.

Note: Before each solo, there will be scale diagrams of the scales used in that solo. The written music in the solos may not adhere strictly to these fingerings, but they provide a good, solid foundation for your own improvisations. In many cases, these are extended fingerings, meaning they show different places that you can play the same notes (for example, the G Harmonic Minor scale to the right). On the CD, you will hear the solo once, then the lead guitar will drop out and the rest of the band will play through the form one more time as a backing track for you to improvise over.

B♭ Major Scale

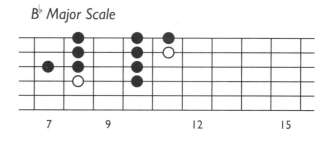

G Harmonic Minor Scale

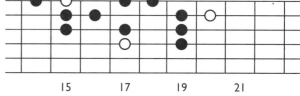

Salsa Solo

(continued on next page)

Play one octave higher than written

G Harmonic Minor scale

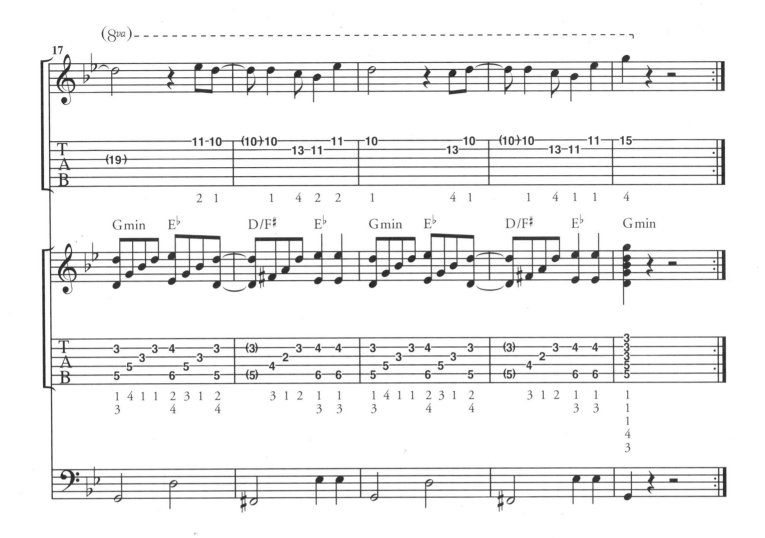

Tito Puente (1923–2000) was a charismatic bandleader who helped popularize the salsa style. He directed the band from behind the timbales with a relaxed yet showy style. His composition "Oye Como Va" was a hit song for the Latin-rock group Santana. Puente was the recipient of six Grammy awards, including special recognition for his lifetime achievement.

Rumba

The Cuban rumba comes from a folkloric dance tradition. There are three styles of rumba: *yambu, columbia,* and *guaguancó.* The guaguancó is the most popular of the three styles. We will look at it in the next chapter. For now, we will focus on the more traditional rumba, which is a bit slower than the guaguancó.

As we learned on page 15, the rumba has its own clave and it is usually in 3-2 form. Here it is to refresh your memory.

Rumba Clave

As you can see, this clave is more syncopated than the son clave. The rumba is a highly syncopated style of music that is not easily mastered. It takes a lot of listening and practicing to feel comfortable with this style. It's best to practice with your metronome or drum machine set to this 3-2 rumba clave. To the right are some rumba recordings and artists to check out.

> ### *Suggested Listening*
>
> Somos Amigos—*Somos Amigos*
> (Camajan Records, 2002)
>
> Eddie Palmieri—*Eddie Palmieri's Suert la Lengua*
> (Charly Records, 2006)
>
> Rumbajazz—*Tribute to Chombo*
> (Sunnyside, 2000)

Rumba Accompaniment

Below is an example of a rumba part played with octaves and arpeggios. Notice the slick voice leading, keeping the 3rd of the C7 chord (E) as the 7th of the F Major chord (E).

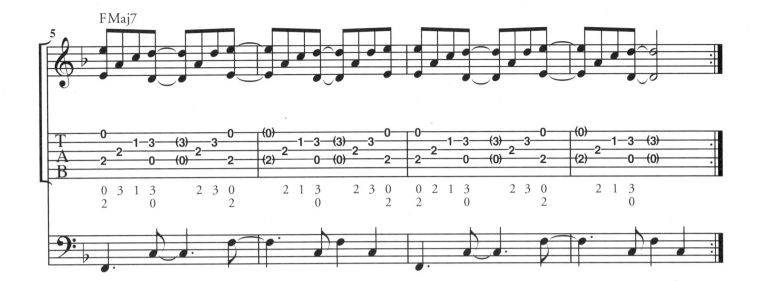

This next example features a *modal chord progression*, a series of chords based on a mode rather than a major or harmonic minor scale. The mode used is the Aeolian mode, or natural minor, with Dmin as the i chord and Amin as the minor v chord. The bass is playing a D Aeolian vamp. Notice that the chords are playing the rhythm of the clave.

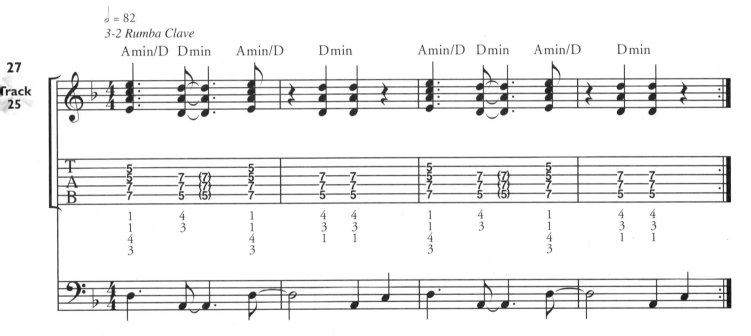

Rumba Solo

On the next page is an example featuring the two rumba accompaniment patterns we just looked at plus a single-note improvisation over the top of them. The solo line is *sequential,* meaning it features a repeated pattern that changes pitch.

The C Mixolydian mode (1–2–3–4–5–6–♭7) is used in the first half of this solo, and the D Aeolian Mode (1–2–♭3–4–5–♭6–♭7), otherwise known as the Natural Minor scale, is used in the second half. Notice that in the second half, the sequential pattern focuses on the 9th and 3rd of the D Minor chord. (See right for scale fingerings.)

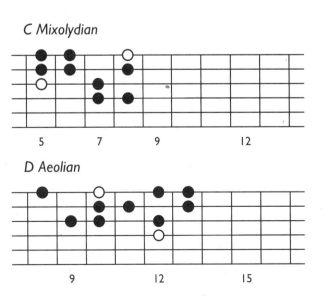

C Mixolydian

D Aeolian

Rumba Solo

Guaguancó

The guaguancó is the more modern form of the three rumba styles. It is the most guitar-friendly rumba style as it is influenced by flamenco music. The guaguancó is usually played in a 3-2 rumba clave. The tempos used for the guaguancó vary from slow to fast, but it is most often associated with brighter tempos. It may be easiest to think of the guaguancó as a faster-paced rumba. While this is not always the case, it serves as a good rule of thumb. To the right are some guaguancó recordings and artists to check out.

Suggested Listening

Eddie Palmieri—*The Best of Eddie Palmieri* (Charly Records, 2006)

Ray Barretto—*The Essential Ray Barretto: A Man and His Music* (Emusica Records, 2007)

Tito Puente—*Dance Mania* (Sony Music, 2009)

Guaguancó Accompaniment

Below is a single-note guaguancó accompaniment pattern. Notice how the first measure of each phrase is more syncopated than the second. This coincides with the "3" side of the rumba clave.

This next example is a chordal guaguancó pattern. Even though there are two notes played at a time (these are referred to as *double stops*) the harmony is strongly suggested over the static bass vamp. The implied chord changes are indicated above the double stops.

Guaguancó Solo

The extended example on the next page features the two accompaniment patterns we just looked at plus a single-note improvisation over the top of them.

The first half of the improvisation uses a G Major scale pattern that sits nicely over the harmony and clave. The second half features a more aggressive, syncopated octave figure taken from the notes of a G13 arpeggio (1–3–5–♭7–9–13). (See diagrams to the right.)

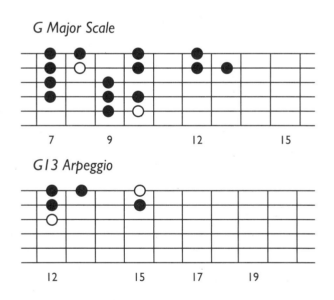

Guaguancó Solo

G13 arpeggio octave figure

Cha-Cha

The cha-cha got its name from the violinist Enrique Jorrín. He named it after the sound the people's feet made while performing this dance. Cha-cha originated from a section of the danzón, which eventually became its own style. In the 1950s, the cha-cha dance craze swept through New York and Cuba.

The cha-cha is known for its simple chord movements, usually iimin7–V7 or iimin7–V7–I. The stepwise connection of the 7th of the iimin7 to the 3rd of the V7 is another example of how guide tones can be used to create smooth chord connections. To the right are some cha-cha recordings and artists to check out.

Suggested Listening

Santana—"Oye Como Va" from *The Best of Santana* (Sony Music, 1998). This song was written by Tito Puente, who also has recorded various versions.

Orquesta Aragón—*Grandes Hits Con La Orquestra Aragon* (Egrem, 1999)

Cal Tjader—*The Ultimate Cal Tjader* (Verve, 1999)

Cha-Cha Accompaniment

Below is a single-note cha-cha accompaniment pattern. Notice that the chord connections between Gmin7–C7 and Amin7–D7 are made by half steps.

The chordal example below is in an older style of the cha-cha, with an almost strumming quality to it. Notice again the smooth chord connections between the minor and dominant chords.

Cha-Cha Solo

On the next page is an example featuring both of the cha-cha accompaniment patterns we just looked at plus a single-note improvisation over the top of them.

The first half features double stops that outline the Gmin to C7 harmony. There is also a little "turn" in bar 4 that complements the accompaniment. The second half features a long descending sequence that sounds like a minor version of the song "Blue Moon." Notice the leading tone (F#) in the 14th bar to emphasize the G Minor tonality. This solo is based more on chord arpeggios than scales. Minor 7th arpeggios consist of chord tones 1–♭3–5–♭7; dominant 7th arpeggios are 1–3–5–♭7; and dominant 9th arpeggios are 1–3–5–♭7–9.

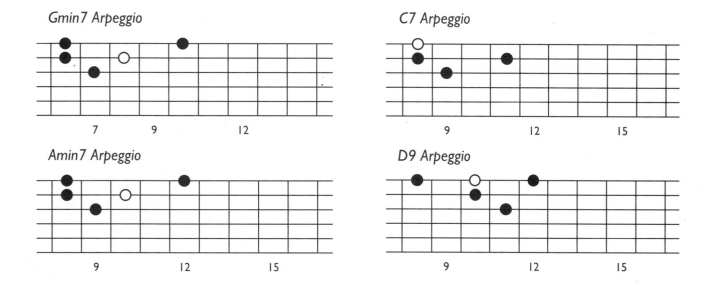

Track 32 ‎ ‎ *Cha-Cha Solo*

Mambo

The first mambo was written in 1938 by two brothers—Orestes and Israel "Cachao" López. Orestes was a multi-instrumentalist and bandleader, while Israel was a bassist and composer. They added a vamp section to a danzón and called it "mambo." This mambo section was a vamp for soloing. The Cuban bandleader Pérez Prado made the mambo an international sensation. He is regarded as the "King of Mambo." His song "Mambo No. 5" has been at the top of the charts since it was first recorded in 1949. To the right are some mambo recordings and artists to check out.

Suggested Listening

Machito & His Afro-Cuban Orchestra—*Mambo Mucho Mambo: The Complete Columbia Masters* (Columbia, 2002)

Pérez Prado—*The Best of Perez Prado* (RCA, 2006)

Tito Puente—*Dance Mania* (Legacy Edition, Sony Music Entertainment, 2009)

Mambo Accompaniment

Following is an example of a single-note mambo pattern. This pattern is four bars long. Remember, however, that the rhythmic concept (based on the 2-3 son clave) is still two bars long.

This next example is a chordal montuno over a G vamp. The chord symbols above the vamp indicate the sound of the chord being played. The F/G chord (the G in the bass is being played by the bassist) creates a G9sus4 sound (C is the 4th of G, F is the ♭7th, and A is the 9th). The line being played by the bassist is a *tumbao,* which is a bass pattern known for its avoidance of the downbeat.

Mambo Solo

On the next page is an example featuring both of the mambo patterns we just covered, plus a single-note improvisation over the top of them.

The first half of the solo starts on the 9th (D) of the Cmin7 chord. This line is four bars long and coincides with the four-bar chordal pattern. This line is diatonic and uses the notes of the B♭ Major scale. However, it still emphasizes the chord tones of the harmonic progression. The first half ends with a rhythmic flourish that becomes the *motif,* or theme, of the second half of the solo. This motif is taken from the F Mixolydian mode and emphasizes the root (F) and 5th (C) of the F chord.

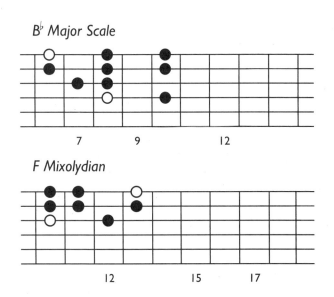

Songo

The songo style was developed in the 1970s by bassist Juan Formell and his group Los Van Van. Songo music is a fusion of the son style with American rock and popular music. It was the first Afro-Cuban style to use drumset. The guitar in this style varies wildly from a distorted rock sound to funk comping, montunos, and single-note vamps. To the right is a list of songo recordings to check out.

Suggested Listening

Juan Formell y Los Van Van—
   Arrasando (Planet Records, 2009)
   The Best of Los Van Van (Egrem, 1997)

Guaco—*Guaco: La Historia 1980–2000*
(Digitalpressure/Latin World Productions, 2002)

Songo Accompaniment

Below is an example of a single-note songo pattern. It is rather simple but works well with the bass part. The tempo is lively, with the half note at 100 beats per minute.

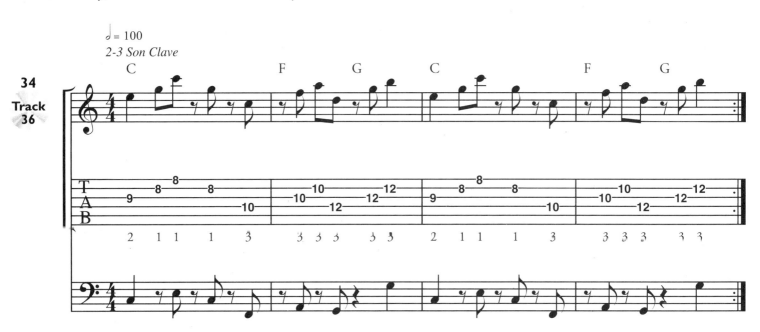

Following is a chordal example of the songo style. Notice the clave is 3-2.

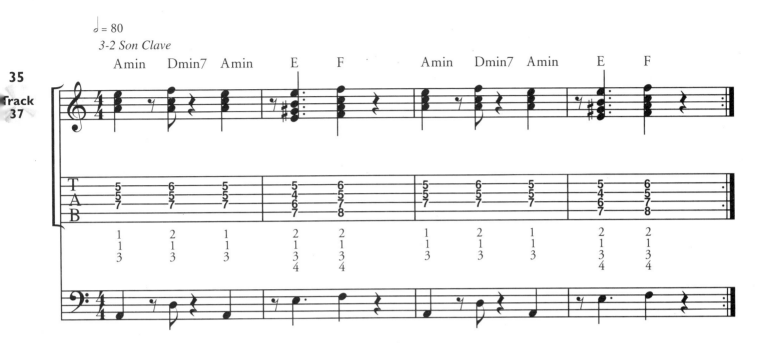

Songo Solo

On the following page is an example that features both of the songo patterns we just covered, plus a single-note improvise over the top of them. Notice that the clave "flips" from 2-3 to 3-2 in the middle of the piece. This is typical of the more modern Afro-Cuban music.

The first half of the solo centers on the 5th (G) of the home key (C) and takes its notes from the C Major scale. The second half has more of a modern blues feel. It switches to an A Harmonic Minor tonality until measure 15, where there is an A Minor Pentatonic run. (The minor pentatonic scale consists of scale degrees 1–$\flat$3–4–5–$\flat$7.)

C Major Scale

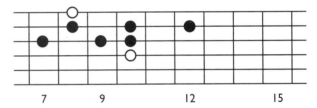

A Harmonic Minor Scale

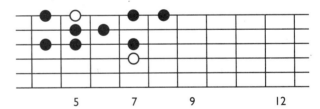

A Minor Pentatonic Scale

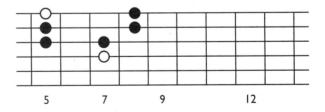

3-2 Son Clave

A Harmonic Minor scale

A Minor Pentatonic run

Mozambique

This lively style of Afro-Cuban music came from the street carnivals, or *comparas* as they are called in Cuba. The tempos are bright and the syncopation is rather complex. The original mozambique is said to have used 16 drums to present the style correctly. Pedro Izquierdo, known professionally as "Pello el Afrokán," is credited with the introduction of the mozambique to the larger public during a TV broadcast in 1963. Pello's composition "Maria Caracoles" was a huge hit and has been covered by artists such as Eddie Palmieri and Carlos Santana. To the right is a list of mozambique recordings to listen to.

Mozambique Accompaniment

Below is an example of a single-note mozambique montuno. Notice the familiar octaves at the start of each phrase and how they move by step to connect the chord changes. You should also note that the clave is a 3-2 rumba.

Below is a chordal mozambique pattern adapted from the piano. Like the previous example, it is also over a 3-2 rumba clave. Notice how beat 4 of the second and fourth bars anticipates the home chord (G) of the progression. A lot of Latin styles resolve to the I chord on beat 4, the way that other styles resolve on beat 1.

Mozambique Solo

On the following page is an example featuring both of the mozambique patterns we just covered, plus a single-note improvisation over the top of them. The solo follows the 3-2 rumba clave, with the emphasis being placed on the syncopation on the "3" side of the clave.

The first half of the solo starts on the "and" of beat 1. There is a four-bar line that ends on the major 7th (F#) of the G Major chord. A similar pattern is used for the next four bars, using more syncopation and ending on the 3rd (B) of the G Major chord. The second half of the solo revolves around the 5th (D) of the home key (G) and then the root (G). This *improv* (as an improvisation, or solo, is sometimes called) is taken from the notes of the G Major scale.

G Major Scale

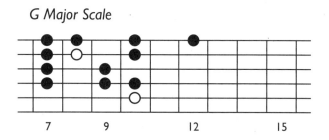

Track 41 Mozambique Solo

*Pianist, composer, and bandleader **Eddie Palmieri** (b. 1936) is known as the "Sun of Latin Music." His bands have created some of the finest and most sophisticated Latin dance music around. Still, Eddie has never been a slave to a single style, and his career has been marked by constant musical growth and exploration. Among his awards and honors are a number of Grammy awards, including the first-ever Grammy awarded in the category of Best Latin Album.*

Chapter 6: Brazil

The music of Brazil comes from a mix of various regional styles influenced by African, European, and the native peoples of the region. With over 500 years of history, Brazilian music has developed many original styles. With the advent of accessibility to radio in the 1930s, popular Brazilian music spread across the country. This music was dominated by female singers, with Carmen Miranda being the most successful of all. Carmen Miranda reached international fame and eventually became a Hollywood movie star. In the 1950s, a slower version of samba was fused with jazz harmonies to create the bossa nova.

It is debatable whether there are claves associated with Brazilian music. However, it is worth noting two rhythms that are often referred to as the "Brazilian clave" (see page 64) and the "bossa clave" (page 68).

BRAZIL

Choro

In Portuguese, the word *choro* means "cry." In traditional Brazilian music, choro refers to a small musical group made up of flute, *violão* (a seven-string nylon guitar with a low B), *cavaquinho* (small, four-string guitar adapted from the ukulele), and *pandeiro* (a percussion instrument similar to the tambourine, played on the lap). The style originated at the turn of the 20th century in Rio de Janeiro. The advent of radio made this music very popular. The choro is known for its fast tempos and virtuosic playing. To the right are some choro recordings for you to check out.

Suggested Listening

Pixinguinha—*Latin Jazz Roots* (Iris Music, 2002)

Jacob do Bandolim—*The Music of Brazil* (Black Round Records, 2009)

Waldir Silva—*Nos Tempos de Ernesto Nazareth E Zequinha de Abreu* (Movie Play Brazil, 2002)

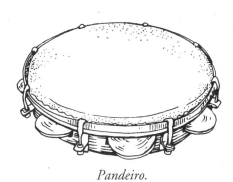

Pandeiro.

Cavaquinho.

Choro Accompaniment

The following examples are written in $\frac{4}{4}$ for easier reading but are played with a "2" feel.

Below, the guitar is copying the rhythm of the pandeiro. This is a typical choro rhythm.

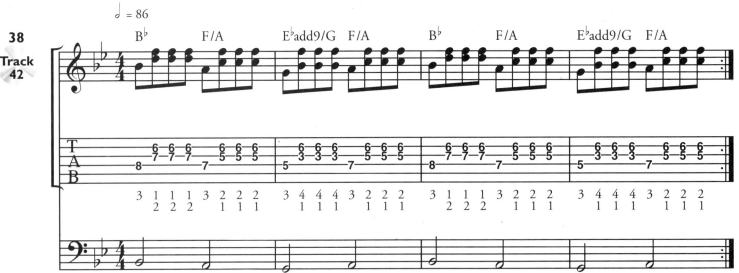

The next example emphasizes the syncopation by removing the downbeats of the chords.

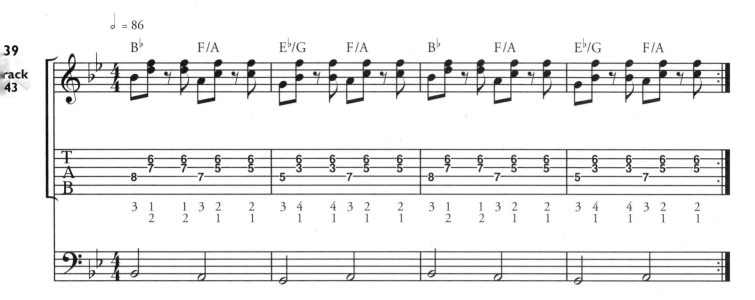

Below is an arpeggiated version of the pattern above.

This next example has a typical choro guitar rhythm. It is on a minor chord progression and in a different *register* (pitch range) than the examples on the previous pages.

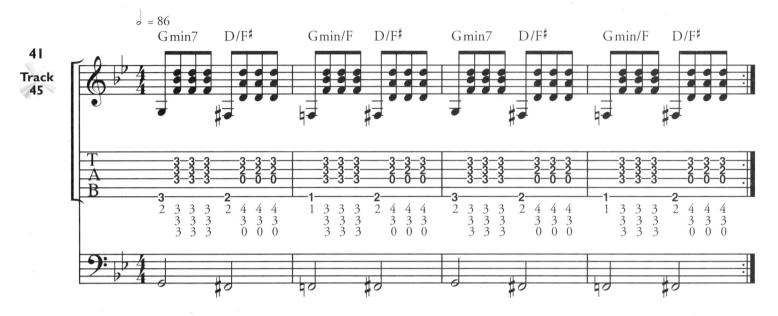

The next example emphasizes the syncopation by removing the downbeats of the chords.

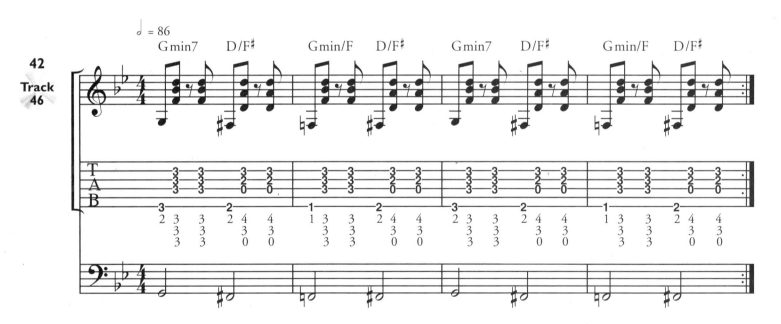

This final accompaniment example is an arpeggiated version of the pattern on the previous page.

Choro Solo

On the next page is an example featuring both types of choro patterns that we just covered, plus a single-note improvisation over the top of them. The first part of the improv starts with a three-note *pickup*. (A pickup refers to notes that occur before the first full measure of music.) This is typical in the choro style. There are also *ornamental turns* in bars 3, 5, and 13. An ornamental turn is an embellishment that involves surrounding a main note with the notes directly above and below it.

The first half of the solo is based on the B♭ Major scale. The second half of the solo is based on the G Harmonic Minor scale and starts with a quick quote from the famous choro song "Tico-Tico."

B♭ Major Scale

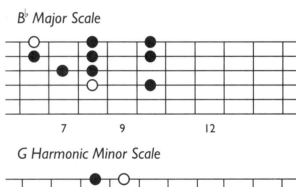

G Harmonic Minor Scale

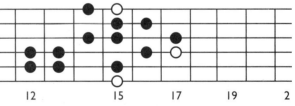

Samba

At the beginning of the 20th century, the samba style evolved from the choro, originating in Rio de Janeiro. As with most of the musical styles in this book, the samba has its origins in dance. In the 1930s, samba music was spread by the advent of radio in Brazil.

Since its original inception, the samba has splintered off into various subgroups. We will look first at the traditional samba. The original samba did not have guitar; it used the cavaquinho. To the right is a list of samba recordings for you to check out.

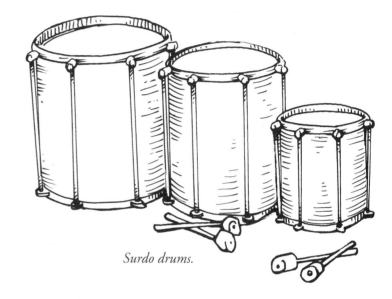

Suggested Listening

Romero Lubambo—*Rio de Janeiro Underground* (441 Records, 2003)

Marisa Monte—*Universo ao Meu Redor* (Monte Criacao E Producao LTD, 2006)

Trio da Paz—*Somewhere* (Blue Toucan Music, 2006)

Samba Accompaniment

The following examples are written in $\frac{4}{4}$ for easier reading but should be played with a "2" feel.

This first example is a basic samba pattern on a I–ii–V chord progression. The single bass note is emulating the low *surdo* drum (a large bass drum used in Brazilian music, see right) while the upper chord structure is emulating the cavaquinho.

Surdo drums.

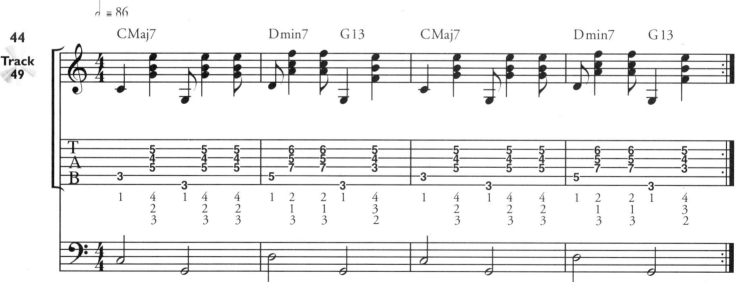

44
Track
49

This next example is the same chord progression but with more syncopation and some ornamentation.

Samba Solo

On the following page is an example that features the two samba patterns we just looked at, plus a single-note improvisation over the top of them. This improv starts on an off-beat (the "and" of beat 1 in the 2nd measure). This use of syncopation is central to the sound of samba. Another rhythmic device used are the quarter note triplets in bars 4, 6, 10, and 11. You can see the development of motifs. The repetition and development of musical motifs help make the improvisation appear as a coherent musical statement. There are ornamental turns in bars 2, 9, and 15. This improvisation is taken from the C Major scale but also targets chord tones in the harmonic progression.

C Major Scale

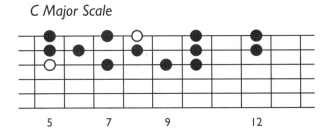

Samba Solo

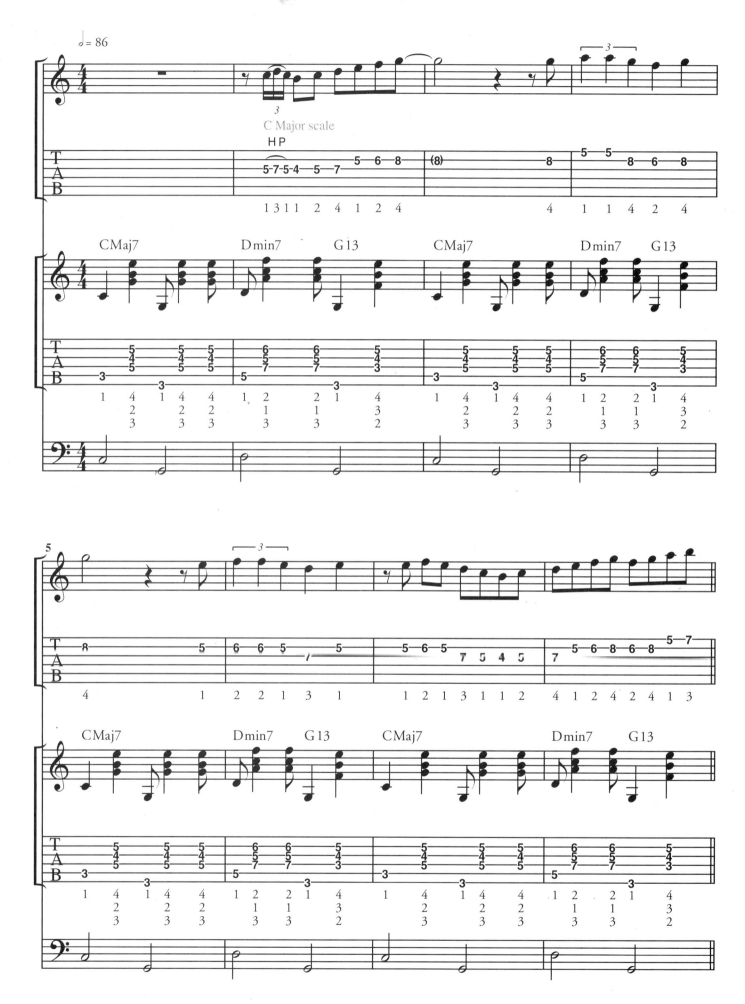

Batucada

Batucada is a sub-style of samba. It originated in the slum area of Rio de Janeiro. The batucada is known for its percussive foundation. It was originally played with just drums and was later adopted as a foundation "groove" for samba music. Many percussion instruments make up the *bateria* (percussion section), which includes the surdo drum, agogo bells, shakers, cuíca, pandeiro, caixa, *apito* (whistle), and güiro. In modern times, the drumset is used to reproduce the sound of the bateria playing the batucada rhythm. To the right are some batucada recordings for you to check out.

Caixa.

Apito.

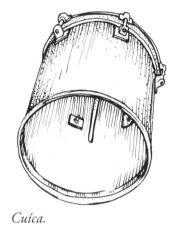

Cuíca.

Güiro.

The following examples are written in $\frac{4}{4}$ for easier reading but should be played with a "2" feel.

The basic batucada pattern is four bars long.

Batucada Pattern

46

Batucada Accompaniment

Below is a basic batucada rhythm pattern adapted for the guitar. It closely follows the rhythmic structure of the example above.

47

Track 52

Below is a more advanced batucada rhythm. Notice the rhythm starts on the pickup ("and" of beat 4) to bar 1.

Batucada Solo

On the following page is an example featuring both of the batucada patterns we just looked at, plus a single-note improvisation over the top of them. The improvisation is very simple, taken from the A Major scale. There are, however, a few things to note. The improvisation starts on the 9th (B) of the AMaj7 chord. The solo follows the rhythm of the batucada. Each of the four-bar phrases end with a sequential line.

A Major Scale

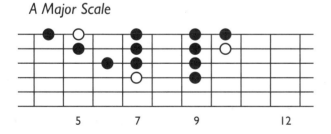

Batucada Solo

Partido Alto

Partido alto is another sub-style of samba. It can be referred to as a certain type of song form, but the term "partido alto" is also used to describe a certain type of rhythm. We will be examining the partido alto as a particular rhythmic sub-style of samba. The rhythm of the partido alto is taken from the agogô bell (see picture below) pattern in the batucada. The partido alto is sometimes referred to as the "Brazilian clave." To the right is a list of recordings for you to check out.

Suggested Listening

João Bosco—*Comissão de Frente* (Universal Music, 1982)

Toots Thielemans—*The Brasil Project* (BMG, 1992)

Airto Moreira—*Life After That* (Narada, 2003)

These are the two Brazilian claves.

The Forward Clave

49
Track 55

The Reverse Clave

50
Track 56

Agogô bells.

Partido Alto Accompaniment

The following examples are written in $\frac{4}{4}$ for easier reading, but they should be played with a "2" feel.

Below is the basic partido alto over a C9 chord.

51
Track 57

Below is the reverse Brazilian clave, or partido alto, with a cycle of chords. This is a more modern harmonic approach to the basic style.

Partido Alto Solo

On the following page is an example with both of the partido alto patterns we just looked at, plus a single-note improvisation over the top of them. The first half of the solo is based on the C Mixolydian mode. It starts on the ♭7 (B♭) of the C9 chord. It's usually a good idea not to start on the root of a chord. In bar 3, we emphasize the tritone (augmented 4th interval) between the 7th (B♭) and the 3rd (E). In bar 8, we play an E♭ note as a passing note to end on the major 7th (E) of the FMaj7 chord that starts the second half of the solo. The second half of the solo winds through the chord progression, always connecting the chord changes by not more than a whole step.

Bossa Nova

The *bossa nova* originated in Rio de Janeiro in the 1950s. It is a combination of a slower samba feel with jazz harmonies. The cool jazz music of the 1950s helped to influence and form the bossa nova style. The first bossa nova recording, a song called "Chega de Saudade," was recorded by Antonio Carlos Jobim and João Gilberto in 1959. In 1963, Stan Getz and João Gilberto released a recording called "The Girl from Ipanema" with Astrud Gilberto (João's wife) singing the vocal. This song became an international hit and made bossa nova the most popular music to come out of Brazil. To the right is a list of bossa nova recordings to check out.

Some musicians identify the two-bar repetitive pattern played on the rim of the snare drum as the bossa nova clave. Here are the two bossa claves.

3-2 Bossa Clave

53

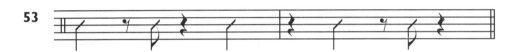

2-3 Bossa Clave

54

The following examples are written in $\frac{4}{4}$ for easier reading, but should be played with a "2" feel.

Bossa Nova Accompaniment

Below is a simple bossa nova pattern.

55
Track
60

Here is a more advanced pattern using the 2-3, or reverse, clave.

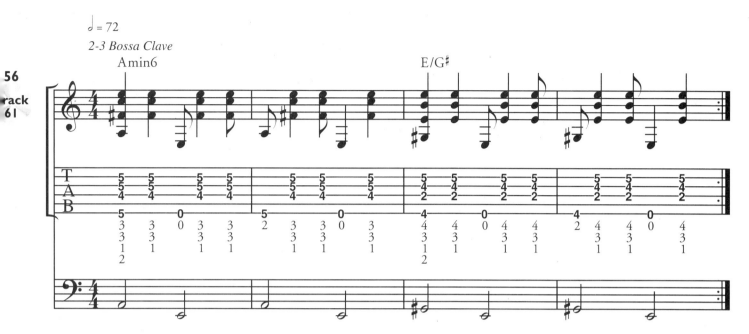

Bossa Nova Solo

On the next page is an example featuring both of the bossa nova patterns we just covered, plus a single-note improvisation over the top of them. The first thing to notice is that both the forward and reverse claves are used in this example. In the first half, we toggle back and forth between C Major and D♭ Major scales. Notice the smooth, step-wise connections between all the chord changes. In addition, we don't stop and restart a line according to the chord changes; all players need to develop the ability to play *across* chord changes without breaking the flow of the line. In the second half of the improv, we emphasize the major 6 (F♯) on the A Minor chord by playing the A Dorian mode (1–2–♭3–4–5–6–♭7) and the major 3rd (G♯) on the E chord by playing the E Major scale. You will notice that we leap across the barline when the chord remains the same, but we always move step-wise across the barline when the chords change.

C Major Scale

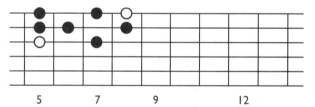

D♭ Major Scale

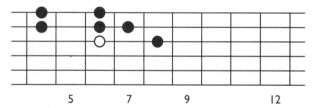

A Dorian

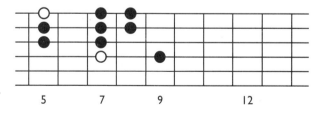

E Major Scale

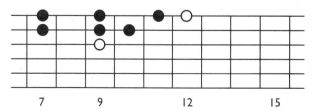

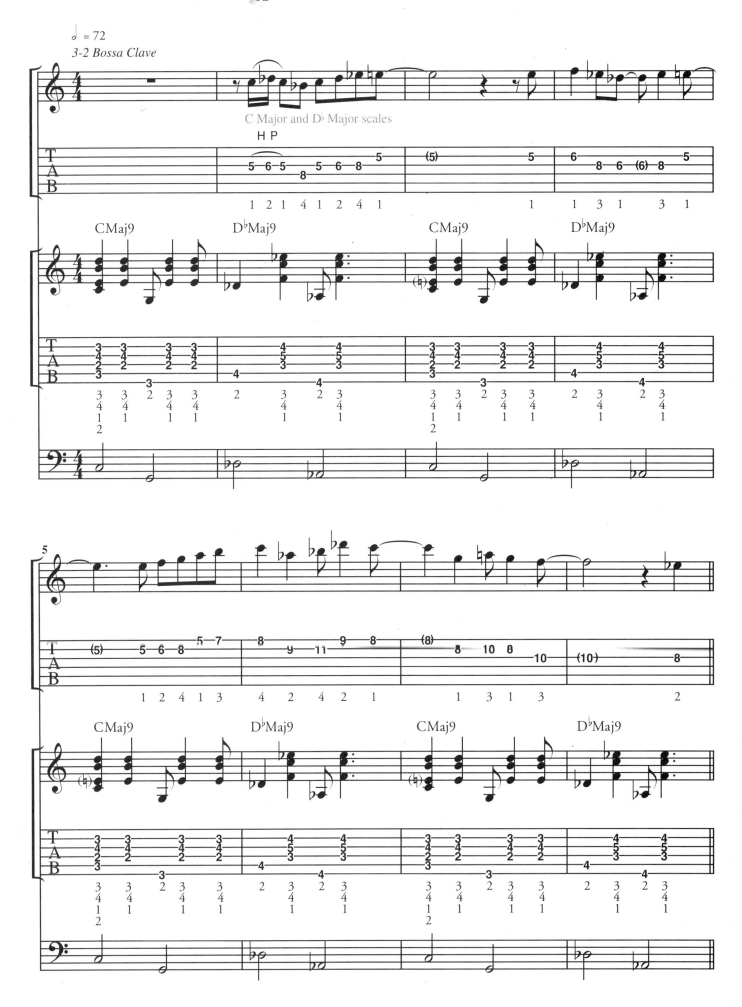

Bossa Nova Solo

Track 62

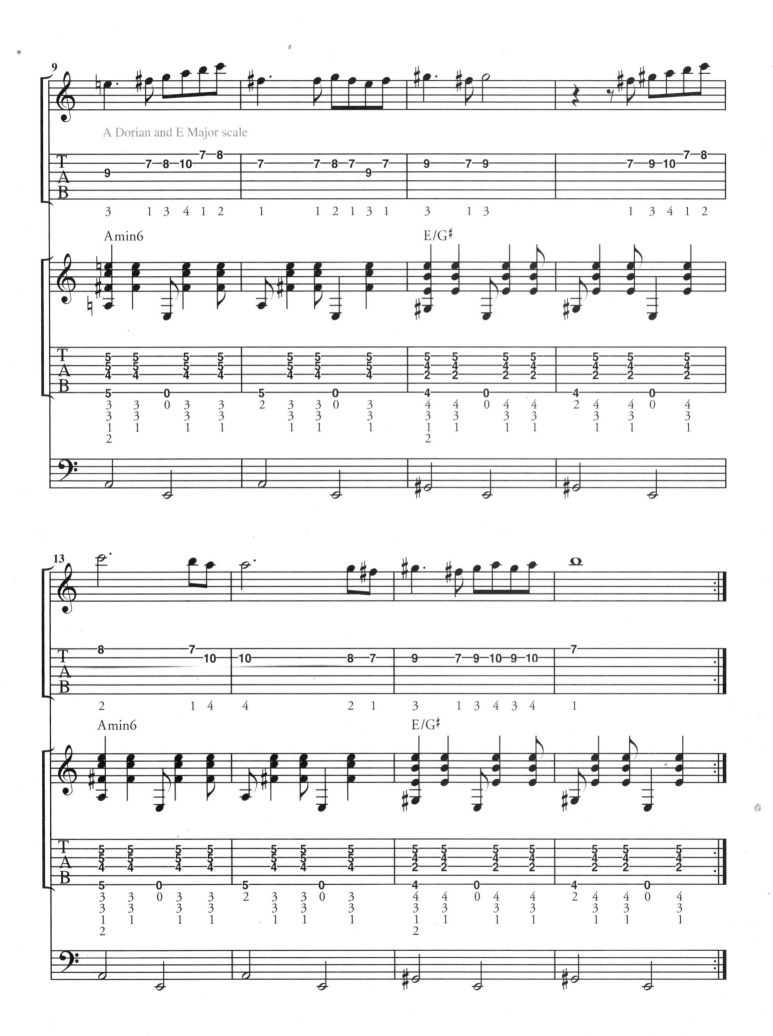

A Dorian and E Major scale

Baião

The *baião* originated in the northeast section of Brazil in the state of Bahia and its surrounding areas. The accordion is the main instrument used in baião, along with flute and the *zabumba drum* (a two-headed drum that is held around the neck by a strap and played with either mallets or sticks, see picture below). The style emerged in the 1940s from a local folk dance. The Brazilian songwriting team of Luiz Gonzaga and Humberto Teixeira developed the baião as it is known today. Check out the list to the right for suggested listening.

The baião rhythm is a one-bar repeated figure usually played over a static bass line creating a sus4 or dominant 7 sound. The melodies are usually based on the Mixolydian or Lydian $^\flat$7 modes. (The Lydian $^\flat$7 mode consists of scale degrees 1–2–3–$^\sharp$4–5–6–$^\flat$7.)

Below is the basic rhythmic pattern.

> ## Suggested Listening
>
> Gilberto Gil—*São João Vivo* (Warner Music Brazil, 2002)
>
> Milton Nascimento—*Courage* (Verve, 1969)
>
> Luiz Gonzaga—*Raizes Nordestinas* (EMI Brazil, 1999)

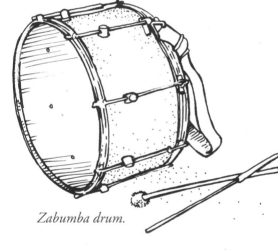

Zabumba drum.

Baião Accompaniment

The following examples are written in $\frac{4}{4}$ for easier reading, but should be played with a "2" feel.

Check out this basic baião pattern for guitar.

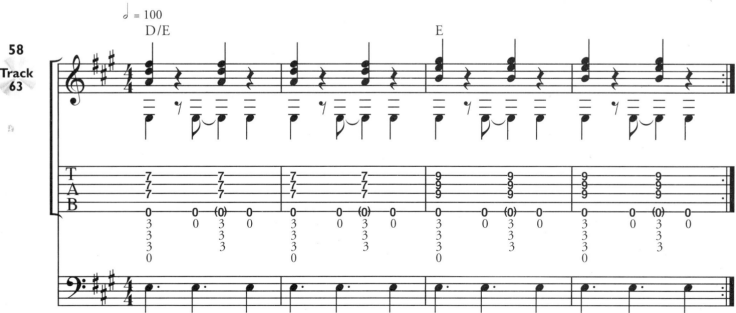

Below is the same chord pattern in an arpeggio style.

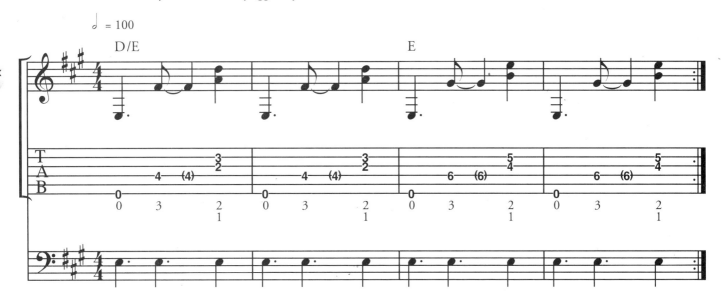

Next is an example where the guitar plays the rhythmic pattern without alternating between the bass notes and chords.

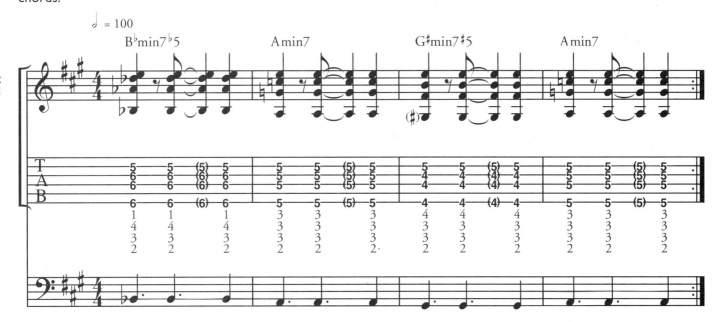

Baião Solo

On the following page is an example with all the baião patterns we just learned, plus a single-note improvisation over the top of them. You will notice that this improvisation has a constant stream of eighth notes. This is typical of the baião style. The improvisation starts with an E Mixolydian mode played scale-wise starting on the ♭7 (D). We also arpeggiate the E7 chord in bars 5 and 6. In the next section, we outline the chords, which creates an E Lydian (1–2–3–♯4–5–6–7), E Minor, and E Major sound over the Bmin7♭5, Amin7, and G♯min7♯5 chords (respectively). The solo finishes with a Lydian sound over the D and E chords and outlines and E Major triad in the last two measures.

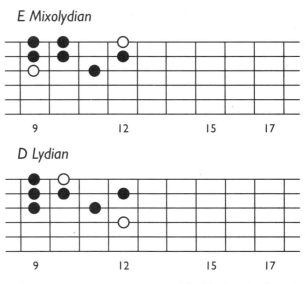

Baião Solo

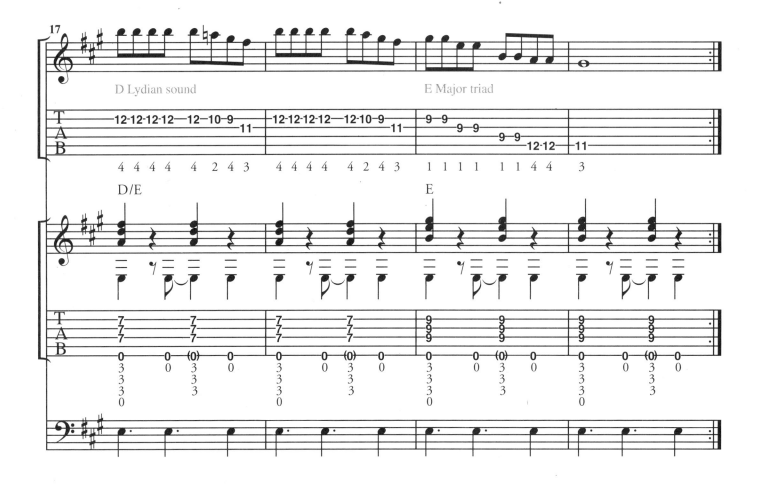

Frevo

The *frevo* style originated around the turn of the 20th century in the Northeastern area of Brazil known as Recife. It was played by military bands, who were based in the city, during ceremonious marches of Carnaval. The original instrumentation was that of the military bands of the time: trumpets, trombone, tuba, clarinet, snare drum, and cymbals. The music was later adapted to smaller groups.

Suggested Listening

Egberto Gismonti—*Solo* (ECM, 1979)

Bico De Chaleira—*Festa: Vol. 1* (Atracao Fonografica, 2008)

Dori Caymmi—*Contemporâneos* (Music Taste, 2003)

This is the basic rhythmic pattern of the frevo. The bassist (or the thumb, when playing without a bassist) keeps a steady half-note pattern underneath this rhythm.

61

Frevo Accompaniment

Below is a typical frevo pattern for guitar. The second measure differs from the rhythm above by syncopating the "and" of beat 1. This is the most common frevo pattern played by guitar and piano.

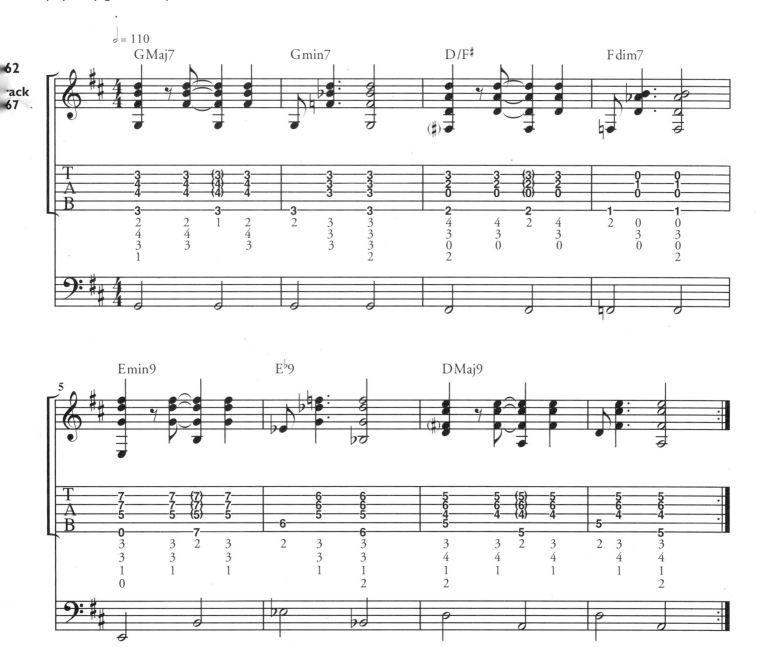

This next pattern is a popular variation that only uses beats 2 and 4. The bass notes are provided by the bass player.

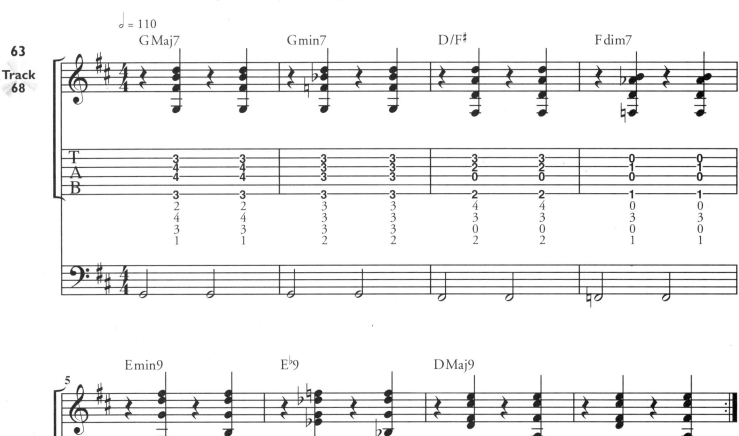

Frevo Solo

On the following page is an example featuring both frevo patterns, plus a single-note improvisation over the top of them. This improv is made up mostly of short phrases that cross the barline and harmonically connect the chord changes by no more than a whole step. The GMaj7 chord is connected to the Gmin7 chord by the major and minor 3rd respectively (B–B♭). The D/F♯ and the Fdim7 are connected via their roots (F♯ on beat 1 of bar 3 and F♯ on the "and" of beat 1 in bar 4). There are smooth connections on every change. This improv is taken from the harmony chords, using the chord tones to create a strong harmonic flow.

Track 69 *Frevo Solo*

(continued on page 80)

Chapter 7: The Dominican Republic

The Dominican Republic is part of an island in the Caribbean called Hispaniola. It shares this island with the country of Haiti. The Dominican Republic, or DR as it is often referred to as, was settled by the Spanish in the 15th century. The Spanish settlers killed off the local people (the Taíno) and eventually brought in slaves from Africa. The resultant cultural mix generated the music styles that will be discussed in this chapter.

The two most well-known music styles from the DR are *merengue* and the more modern *bachata*. Both styles are based on dances that developed in the poorer sections of the DR. Both styles are also known for their unique lyric content.

There is no clave associated with bachata. However, a standard 2-3 and 3-2 son-type clave is used in the merengue style. In the pages that follow, we will just refer to these as "2-3 clave" and "3-2 clave." They are to be played exactly the same as the son claves covered on page 14.

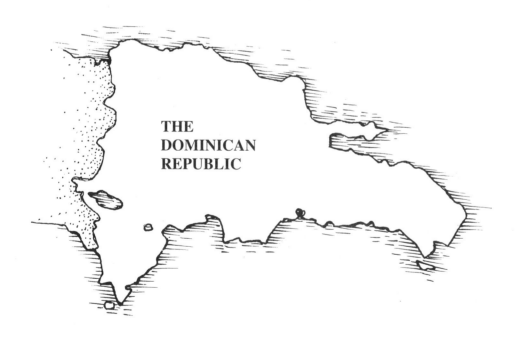

THE
DOMINICAN
REPUBLIC

Merengue

The music most often associated with the Dominican Republic is merengue. This music is characterized by its uptempo rhythm and syncopation. The merengue was developed in the mid-19th century but didn't achieve widespread acceptance until the 1930s. When Rafael Trujillo became the dictator of the DR, he took the music of his lower-class youth, merengue, and made it the dominant musical genre on the island. The advent of radio also helped to spread this music across the island. The suggestive lyrics often found in merengue did not help it gain widespread appeal. Later on, some artists, such as Francisco Ulloa, used socially charged lyrics in merengue.

Suggested Listening

Francisco Ulloa—*Pegaito* (Karen Publishing, 1995)

Johnny Ventura—*10 de Colección* (Sony BMG, 2008)

Various artists—*iTunes Essentials: Merengue* (iTunes, 2009)

Merengue Accompaniment

The example below is in the older style of merengue, which used alternating bass and was less syncopated than the modern merengue style. This pattern is taken from the accordion, which was the dominant instrument in the merengue group, along with the tambora drum and guiro.

Accordion.

Tambora drum.

The example below is in a more modern style like that of singer and bandleader Johnny Ventura. Notice the highly syncopated rhythms.

Merengue Solo

On the following page is an example featuring both of the merengue patterns we just looked at, plus a single-note improvisation over the top of them. Merengue is known for its bright tempos and suggestive lyrics. Because of the bright tempos, its melodies are not as complex. The entire improv is taken from the D Major scale. The first half of the improv is sequential with a whole note followed by a repeated rhythm. You will notice that attention is still given to the larger picture of chord connection and the spelling of the harmonies. The second half of the improv takes the sequence one step further by adding an extra note to the measure with the long tone. This repetition is typical of the merengue style.

D Major Scale

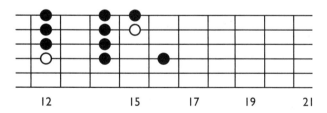

Bachata

The second musical style that emerged from the DR is the bachata. The Bachata started out as a traditional, guitar-oriented music. It was often played in brothels and had a stigma attached to the name (much like the word "jazz" in its early days). After the assassination of Rafael Trujillo in 1961, bachata music took on new meaning. It became the DR's version of the blues. The words in this style tell stories of poverty, jealousy, and fights that occurred in the *barrios,* or neighborhoods. Bachata become known as the music of sorrow.

Suggested Listening

Blas Duran—*El Carnicero* (unknown label, 1991)

Various artists—*Señora Bachata* (Mock and Roll, 2009)

Luis Segura—*El Papa de la Bachata* (Platano Records, 1994)

Bachata Accompaniment

Below is an example of the classic bachata guitar rhythm.

Following is an example of the bachata played in a modern arpeggio style.

Bachata Solo

On the next page is an example featuring both bachata patterns plus a single-note improvisation over the top of them. Since this tempo is slow, the improv can be more intricate. It starts with an ornamentation around the $^\flat 9$ ($B^\flat$) of the A7 chord. The line is taken from the D Harmonic minor scale. This idea is kept as a theme throughout the first half. In the second half, the accompaniment plays single notes so the improv switches to double stops based on the chord tones of each underlying chord. As an improviser, be aware of what the rest of the group is doing. It should influence what you play. Conversely, what you play should influence how the rest of the group accompanies you.

D Harmonic Minor Scale

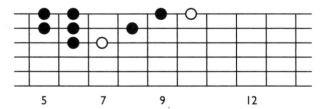

Chapter 8: Trinidad

The Caribbean island of Trinidad saw an influx of Spanish settlers and African slaves in the 1600s. The Spanish took over and marginalized the native population (the Arawak). Later, in 1802, the British claimed the island from Spain. French Creoles also came and settled on the island. In 1834, the island slaves were emancipated. This led to a merging of the various cultures in Trinidad. Between 1845 and the early 20th century, many more immigrants from India, China, Africa, and Portugal came to the island. The *steel pan* (see illustration below) of Trinidad is the result of an evolution from bamboo poles and percussion groups made of pots, pans, and oil drums.

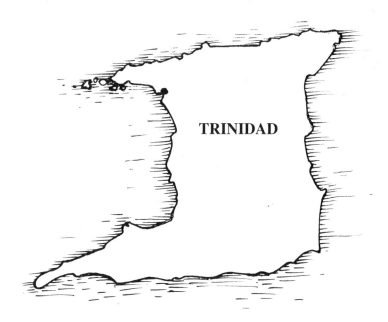

TRINIDAD

Calypso is the most popular music export from Trinidad. The calypso started as a means of musical communication, called *kaiso,* for the African slaves. With the abolition of slavery and the influx of different populations, kaiso developed into calypso.

Soca is another popular dance music from Trinidad. It is a more modern version of calypso.

There is no known clave associated with calypso or soca music.

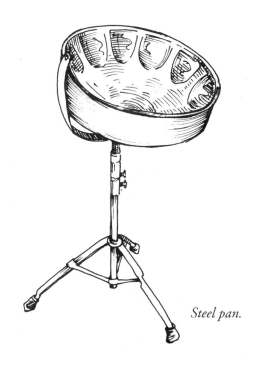

Steel pan.

Calypso

Calypso music started as kaiso, a means for the African slaves of Trinidad, who were not permitted to speak to each other, to communicate. The Spanish controlled the island until the British took over in 1802. In 1834, slavery was abolished. Among the many countries that settled the region, the French had a large impact on the music. The French Creoles brought Mardi Gras/Carnaval to the island. Many of the early calypsos are sung in a French-Creole dialect, or *patois*.

Suggested Listening

Various artists—*The Alan Lomax Collection* (Rounder, 2000)

Various artists—*Calypso: Best of Trinidad* (BMG, 2004)

The Mighty Sparrow—*King Sparrow's Calypso Carnival* (Smithsonian Folkways, 2004; originally released 1959)

The early calypso bands had two distinct forms. One form was a band made up completely of rhythm instruments and singers. The other was a small ensemble of guitar (or guitar-like instrument), bass, light percussion, vocalist, and a clarinet, flute, or saxophone. There are also groups with added violin and piano. We are going to look at the calypso style that incorporated the small ensemble.

PHOTO COURTESY OF THE INSTITUTE OF JAZZ STUDIES, RUTGERS UNIVERSITY

*Known as the "King of Calypso," **Harry Belafonte** (b. 1927) is an American musician, actor, and social activist who popularized the Trinidadian music style of calypso throughout the world in the 1950s.*

Calypso Accompaniment

Following is a basic guitar accompaniment in the calypso style. Notice that the bass plays what jazz musicians would call a "broken two" feel, which alternates between half notes and a walking bass line.

This example should be strummed, not finger-picked.

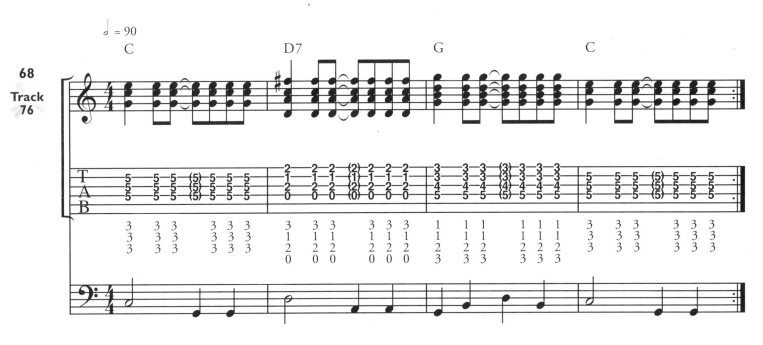

This next example is more advanced, with a "swing feel" to the eighth notes (see page 109). It should be strummed instead of finger-picked.

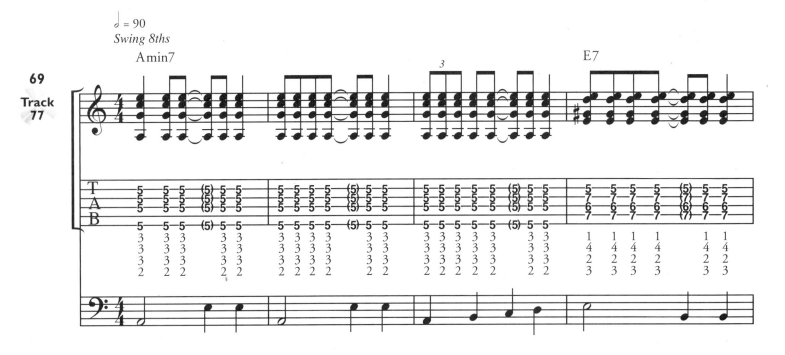

Calypso Solo

On the following page is an example featuring both calypso patterns we just looked at, plus a single-note improvisation over the top of them. The improv is reflective of the simple, lyrical quality of this style of music. In the first half, the melody centers around the 3rd and 7th of the chords. This helps to spell out the harmony and make musical sense of the melodic pattern. The second half of the improv is over the relative minor of C Major (A Minor). The leading tone (G♯) is emphasized on the E7 chord along with the ♭9 (F).

Calypso Solo

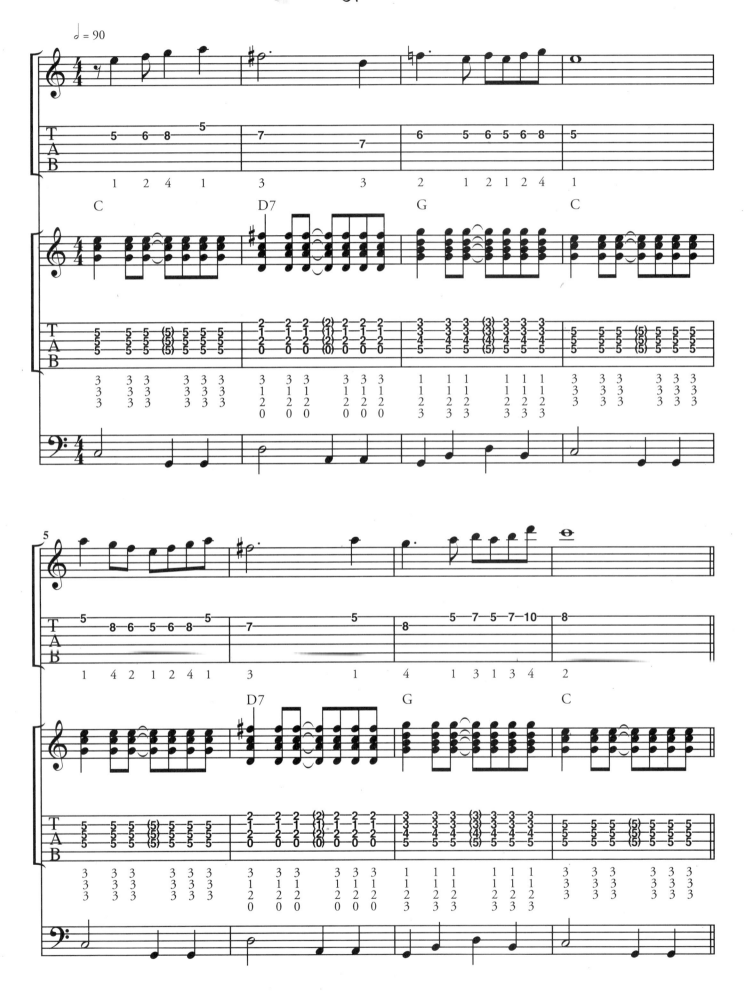

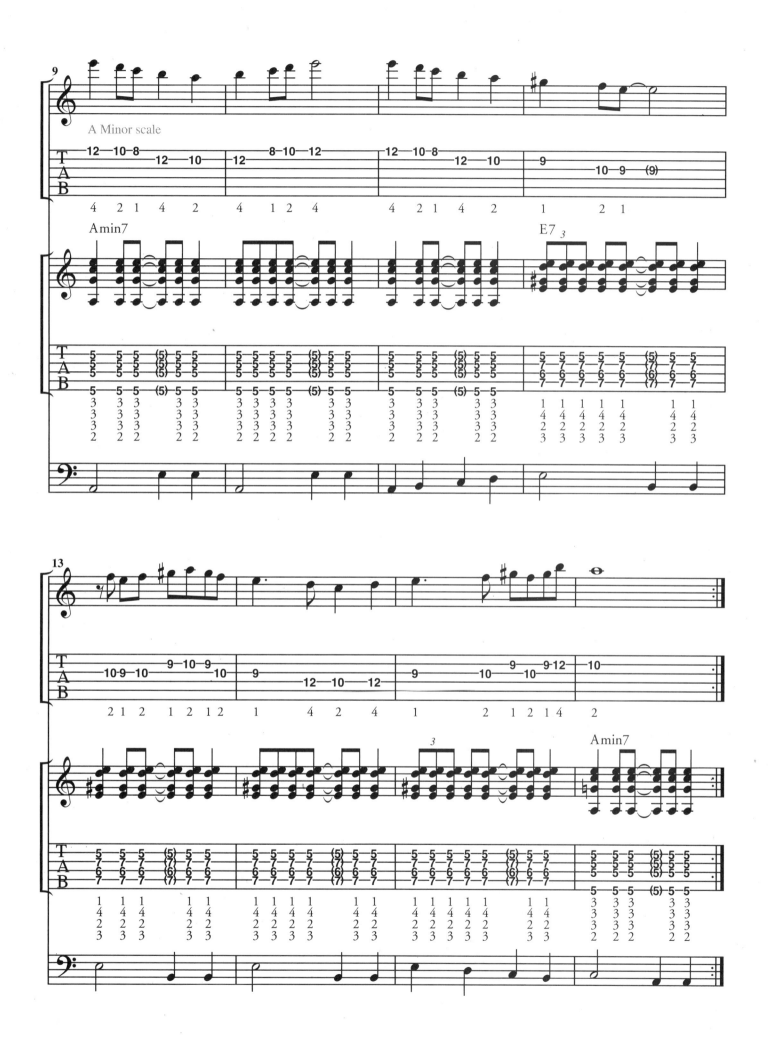

Soca

Soca grew out of calypso to become a popular music style. Soca music is a fusion of calypso with Indian rhythms, combining the musical traditions of the two major ethnic groups of Trinidad and Tobago (the smaller of the two main islands that constitute the Republic of Trinidad and Tobago). The soca style was created by Garfield Blackman, whose stage name was "Lord Shorty." The style was developed in the 1960s and became better known after the success of Lord Shorty's hit song "Indrani."

> ## Suggested Listening
>
> Arrow—*The Best of Arrow* (Red Bullet, 1987)
>
> Lord Kitchener—*Play Mas' with Kitch* (Radiophone Archives, 1968)
>
> Soca Boys—*The Album* (Red Bullet, 1998)

Soca Accompaniment

Soca rhythms are strummed on the guitar, rather than finger-picked.

This first example is the traditional soca guitar rhythm. It is in the style of early soca music. Notice the bass line maintains a steady rhythm as opposed to the "broken two" feel of calypso. This style is best played by strumming with the thumb.

70
Track
79

Here is a more modern strumming pattern in a soca style used by the performer Arrow.

Soca Solo

On the next page is an example with both soca patterns plus a single-note improvisation over the top of them. In the soca style, the trumpet is often the lead instrument. This improv is based on the lines a trumpet would play in this style. All the chord changes are connected by step. The improv is a combination of arpeggios over each chord and repeated scale-type riffs. Even though we are in the key of A Major, the A chord in bar 4 turns dominant (A7) in the second half of the bar. This leads to a smooth connection between the ♭7 of the A chord (G natural) and the 3rd of the D chord (F♯). The D chord feels more like a I chord instead of a IV chord; this process is called *tonicization*.

Soca Solo

Chapter 9: Argentina

The country of Argentina is located in South America. After many defeats by the native peoples, the Spanish finally conquered the country in the late 16th century. The Spanish rule lasted until Napoleon overthrew the Spanish monarchy. It took until the end of the 19th century before Argentina had a stable government. At that point, many immigrants flocked to the country, especially to Buenos Aires.

Tango is the national music of Argentina. The *milonga* was an early music that evolved into the tango soon after the turn of the 20th century. The tango started out as the preferred music of the criminals and gangsters who visited the brothels in Buenos Aires. The dances that arose from this music were a result of the toughness and sexual aggressiveness in the area. The first generation of tango was called *guardia vieja* (the old guard). The tango continues to evolve and remains the most popular music of Argentina.

ARGENTINA

Tango

Tango is a type of music and dance form that originated in Buenos Aires, Argentina. It is a combination of European rhythms brought to the area by various traders and immigrants. The milonga was an early music that evolved into the tango soon after the turn of the 20th century. By the 1930s, the Tango was the dance craze of Buenos Aires. The traditional tango orchestra *(orquestra tipica)* consisted of two violins, piano, double bass, and two *bandoneóns* (an accordion-like instrument; see illustration below). An earlier form of the ensemble was made up of guitar, clarinet, and flute.

Suggested Listening

Francisco Canaro—*The Originals: 1938–1952 Recordings* (YOYO USA, 2006)

Carlos Gardel—*Carlos Gardel En Música Y En Fotos* (YOYO USA, 2006; originally released 1950)

Astor Piazzolla—*The Soul of Tango: Greatest Hits* (Éditions Milan Music, 2000)

Following are the two traditional tango rhythms.

Simple Tango Rhythm

Syncopated Tango Rhythm

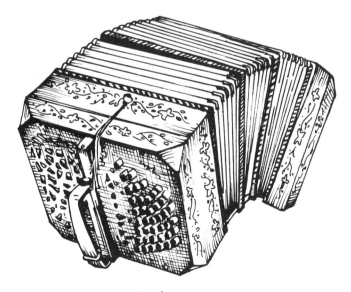

Bandoneón.

Tango Accompaniment

The tango has a strong march-like element. Sometimes, the guitar plays straight quarter notes with the fingers and adds the tango accents with the thumb.

The following examples are written in $\frac{4}{4}$ for easier reading, but they should be played with a "2" feel.

Below is an example of the simple tango rhythm using the thumb to create the accents while the fingers keep straight time with quarter notes.

Here is an example of the more syncopated tango style with the guitar just playing the accents. Notice the bass plays both of the tango rhythms.

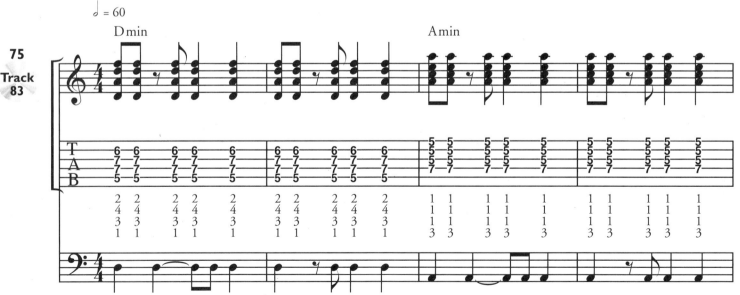

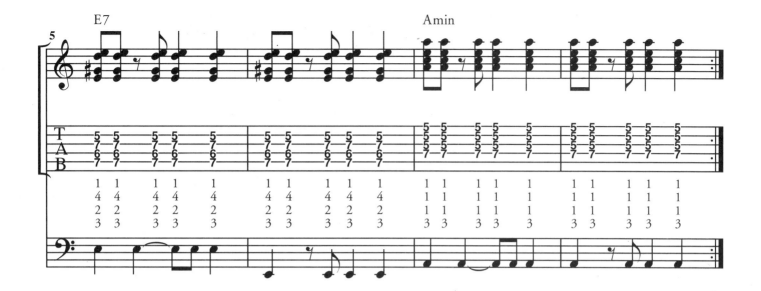

Tango Solo

On the following page is an example featuring both tango patterns and a single-note improvisation over the top of them. The tango is a passionate dance. This improv typifies the ornamentation of melodies used in this music. The technique used here is called *enclosure*. In the pick-up bar, the note E is enclosed on either side by a note one half step away in either direction (D♯ and F). The same technique is applied in the second half of the improv, enclosing the note A. This improv is based more on chord tones than on scales or modes.

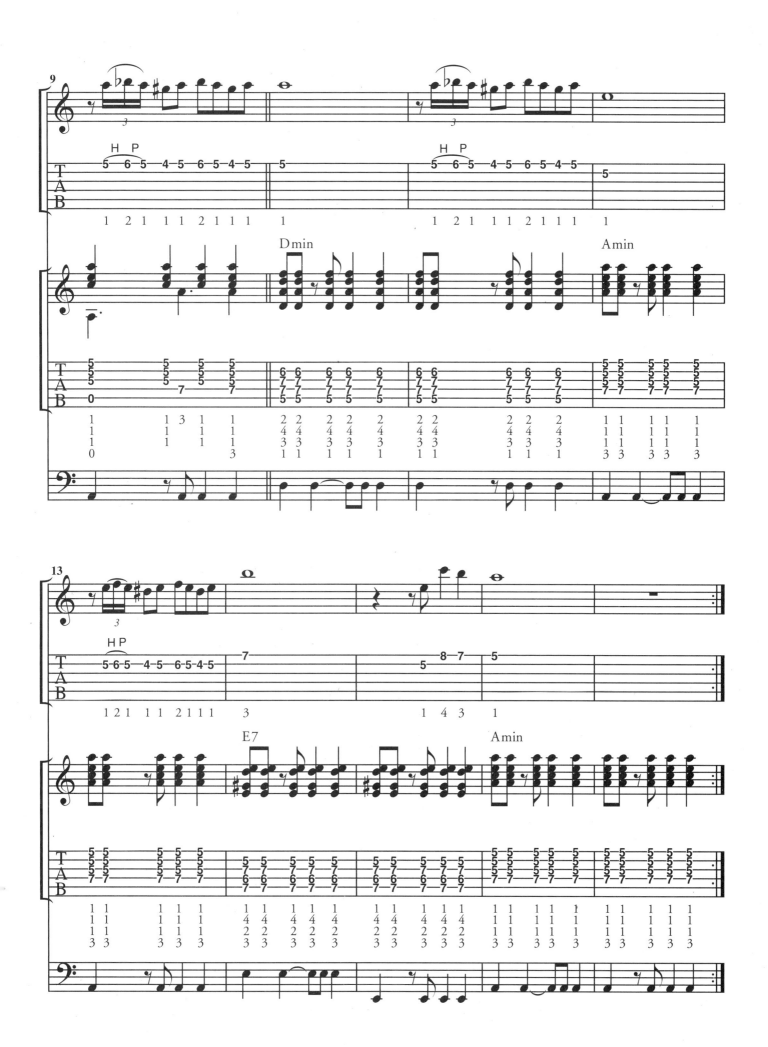

Chapter 10: Mexico

The music of Mexico is quite diverse and has influences from many cultures. The most notable styles of Mexican music share influences with the Amerindian,* European, African, and American cultures. There have been many defining moments in Mexican history, such as the Aztec civilization (13th century), the Spanish colonization (16th century) and subsequent influx of African slaves, Mexico's independence (1810–1821), the Mexican-American War (1846–1848), and the Mexican Revolution in the early 20th century.

Many Mexican songs have become worldwide standards, including "Bésame Mucho," "Cielito Lindo," and "La Bamba."

The four styles discussed in this chapter are *ranchera, mariachi, norteño,* and *tejano.* Each style reflects its own particular regional and cultural influences.

MEXICO

* The term *Amerindian* refers to all the indigenous peoples of North, Central, and South America.

A mariachi group. The mariachi is essentially the Mexican version of the Spanish classical orchestra. The instrumentation includes violins, trumpets, guitar, vihuela, and guitarrón (although since the 1970s, other instruments, like the accordion in the picture above, are occasionally added). The members of the mariachi dress in specific outfits called charros. The mariachi were originally street musicians but are now known for playing weddings and professional engagements. (See page 114.)

Ranchera

The ranchera is part of the traditional music of Mexico. It was developed during the post-revolutionary period. The ranchera themes usually dealt with patriotism and love. They were drawn from traditional rural folklore. The traditional instrumentation includes guitars, violins, trumpets, and (sometimes) accordion. Ranchera songs were usually in major keys and in $\frac{3}{4}$ time, as well as $\frac{4}{4}$.

Suggested Listening

José Alfredo Jiménez—*Las 100 Clasicas, Vol. 1* (BMG, 2000)

Lola Beltrán—*Canta 16 Éxitos de José Alfredo Jiménez* (YOYO USA, 2006)

Cuco Sánchez—*La Gran Coleccion del 60 Aniversario CBS* (SONY BMG, 2007)

Ranchera Accompaniment

Below is a basic ranchera in $\frac{3}{4}$ time. Notice the chord progression uses an alternating bass pattern (root and 5th). Unique to this style is the use of the V chord (G) as a "sub" chord for the C/G.

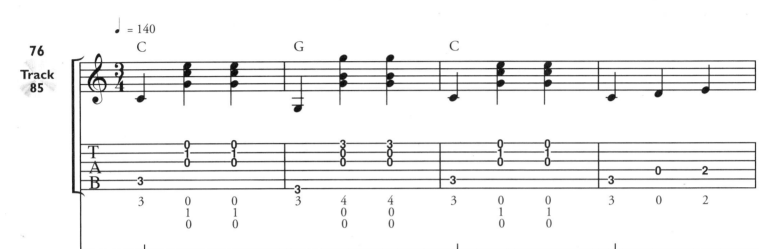

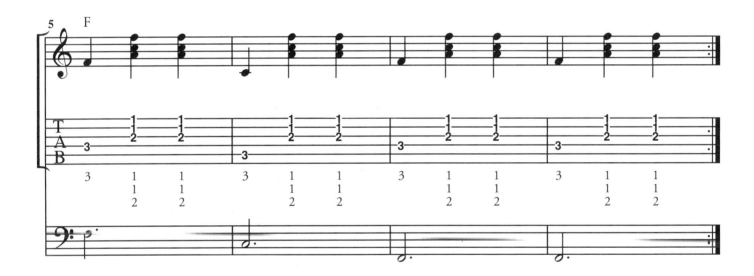

Swing Eighth Notes

The example on the next page uses *swing eighth notes*. The easiest way to achieve the swing-eighth-note feel is to play eighth notes as if they were the first and third note of a triplet.

Below is how swing eighth notes should be played.

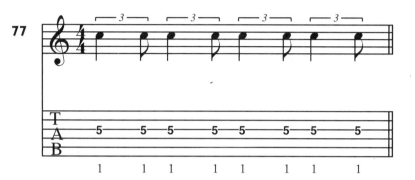

However, they are written as regular eighth notes (to make the music easier to read), with *Swing 8ths* indicated at the beginning.

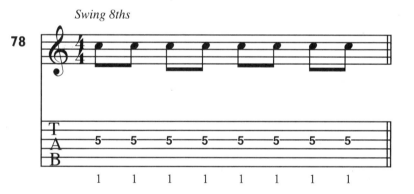

Below is the same ¾ ranchera pattern from page 108, but in a more advanced style. Notice that we are using swing eighth notes.

Below is an example of a basic $\frac{4}{4}$ ranchera. Notice how the combination of chords and an alternating bass figure creates a constant stream of eighth notes. We will not be using swing eighth notes for the following two examples.

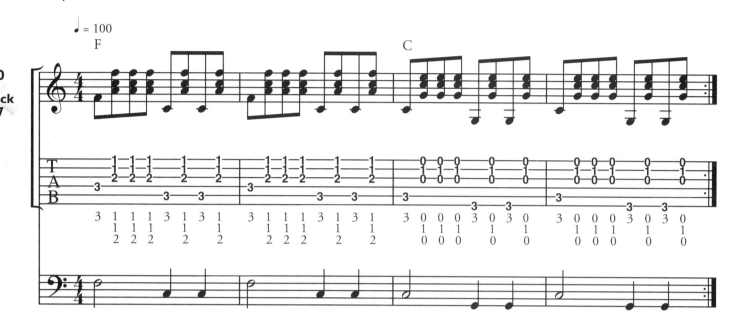

Below is an example of a more advanced $\frac{4}{4}$ ranchera.

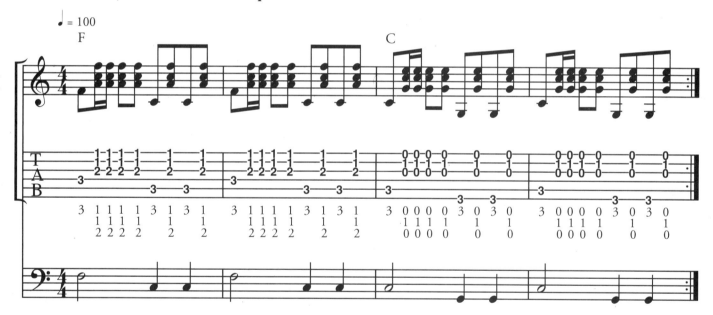

Ranchera Solo

On the following page is an example featuring both of the $\frac{3}{4}$ ranchera patterns we looked at, plus a single-note improvisation over the top of them. The swing eighth notes help give this style its authentic flavor. This entire solo is played using double stops, which is also characteristic of this style. The notes are taken from the C Major scale, although there is a B♭ flat note in bar 6 to enhance the F Major sound. The rhythms are simple and repetitive. The double stops imply the underlying harmony.

C Major Scale

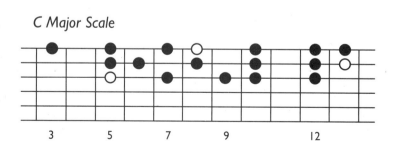

Ranchera Solo

Mariachi

In the early 16th century, the Spanish began to colonize Mexico. With this Spanish colonization came an influx of European instruments that soon replaced many of the traditional native instruments. The known form of mariachi started in the 19th century in the Mexican state of Jalisco. The mariachi is essentially the Mexican version of the Spanish classical orchestra. The instrumentation includes violins, trumpets, guitar, *vihuela* (small, guitar-like instrument), and *guitarrón* (small, acoustic bass guitar). The members of the mariachi dress in specific outfits called *charros* (see photograph on page 107). The mariachi were originally street musicians but are now known for playing weddings and professional engagements.

Suggested Listening

Mariachi Nuevo Tecalitlán—*México y Su Mariachi* (Phonomaster Records, 1998)

Mariachi Vargas de Tecalitlán—*Las Mañanitas* (Peerless, 1998)

Nati Cano—*Viva el Mariachi!* (Smithsonian Folkways, 2002)

Mariachi Accompaniment

Below is an example of the traditional mariachi rhythm in ¾ time. Notice that it is a two-bar pattern similar to the clave concepts in Afro-Cuban music.

✗ = *Chuck*. Unpitched, percussive-sounding attack created by lightly touching the strings with your left hand while strumming with your right.

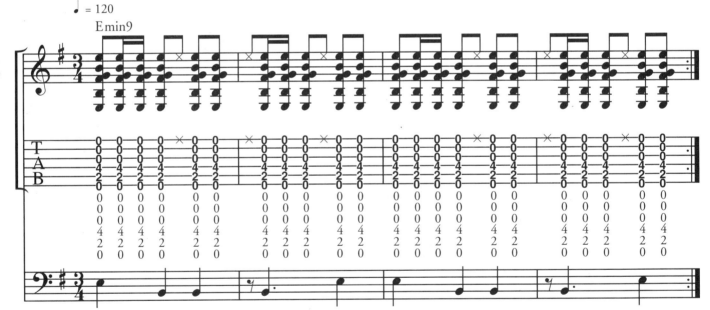

This next example is a *rasgueado* pattern used frequently in mariachi music. The rasgueado is a study unto itself. As applied to the following examples, this technique is executed by using a basic *fan* pattern. This pattern is created by placing your thumb on the 6th string and "fanning" out your fingers, from a closed-fist position, starting with your 4th finger. You fan your fingers out—4th, 3rd, 2nd, and 1st—to create this classic Spanish flamenco sound. In the music, the rasgueado technique is indicated with slash marks through the stems of the notes and above the TAB.

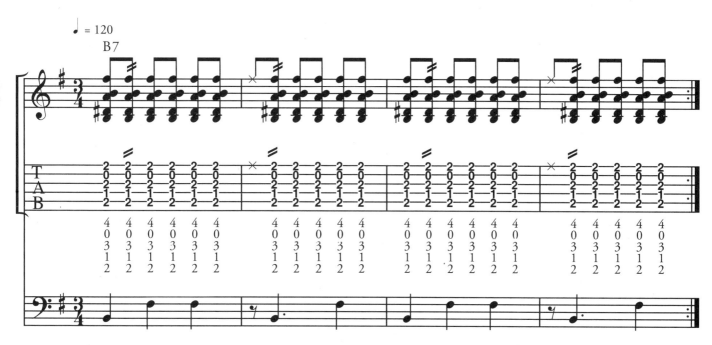

Mariachi Solo

On the next page is an example featuring both of the mariachi patterns plus a single-note improvisation over the top of them. In mariachi music, the violin and/or trumpet would play the lead lines. They are usually based on classical principles. In this improv, the line starts with an imitation of the guitar rhythm. In bars 4 and 6, the line rests on the 9th (F♯) of the Emin chord. The E Natural Minor scale is used throughout the first half of the improv. The second half of the improv makes use of the leading tone (D♯) to emphasize the B7 chord and creates an E Harmonic Minor sound.

E Natural Minor Scale

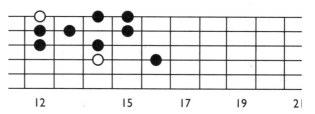

E Harmonic Minor Scale

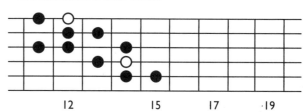

Mariachi Solo

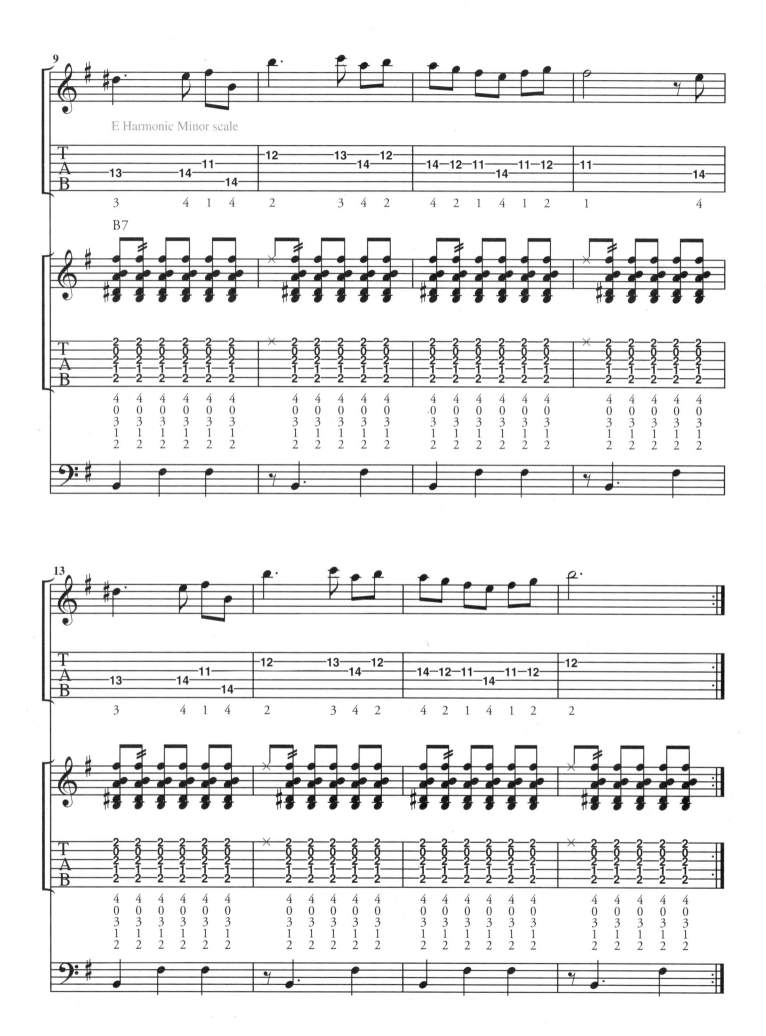

E Harmonic Minor scale

Norteño/Conjunto

Norteño means "northern" in Spanish. During the late 19th century, people from Germany and Czechoslovakia came to northern Mexico, bringing with them the accordion. Together with the *bajo sexto* (a 12-string Mexican guitar; see illustration on next page), these instruments formed the basis of a new genre of music called *norteño*, or "conjunto," which evolved out of the ranchera style. Traditional norteño bands played polkas (European) and rancheras (Mexican). The modernization of the norteño in the 1970s and 1980s introduced electric bass guitar, saxophone, and drumset to the music.

Norteño Accompaniment

Following is a traditional norteño as played by the bajo sexto. Although the traditional norteño groups did not feature bass, we have included a bass part for a fuller sound.

84
Track 93

Below is a more modern norteño.

Norteño Solo

On the next page is an example with both of the norteño patterns plus a single-note improvisation over the top of them. The first half of the improv revolves around the chord-tone half notes: D on the G chord—C, E, and G on the C chord. Notice in the first half that we have left out the bass part, which is typical of the traditional norteño style. The repetitive nature of the improv is also typical of this style. The second half goes into double stops in 3rds that would usually be played by the trumpets. These double stops are more scale-like and are taken from the C Major scale.

Bajo sexto.

Norteño Solo

Tejano

In the 1950s, norteño music branched off into a new popular music called *tejano*. This music, which is also known as *Tex-Mex*, was heavily influenced by American rock and jazz music. Electric guitars and drums were added to the traditional norteño bands.

The tejano style has evolved into three types: *conjunto* (traditional norteño instrumentation), *orchestra* (bass, drumset, electric guitar, and synthesizer/accordion), and *modern* (same instrumentation as orchestra but with emphasis on synthesizer).

Suggested Listening

Esteban "Steve" Jordan—*The Many Sounds of Esteban "Steve" Jordan*
(Arhoolie Productions, 1995)

Ruben y Alfonso Ramos—*Back to Back Again*
(Hacienda Records, 2006)

La Mafia—*30 Exitos Insuperables* (EMI, 2003)

The conjunto style is very similar to the previously studied norteño. This modern style is like contemporary pop music. For these reasons, we will look at the modern style, which served as a good fusion of the norteño and American influences.

Tejano Accompaniment

Below is a typical tejano guitar part that would accompany the melody played by accordion and vocalist. You will notice that it is similar to the norteño style but with more single notes and less reliance on bass figures (because of the presence of a bass player in the group).

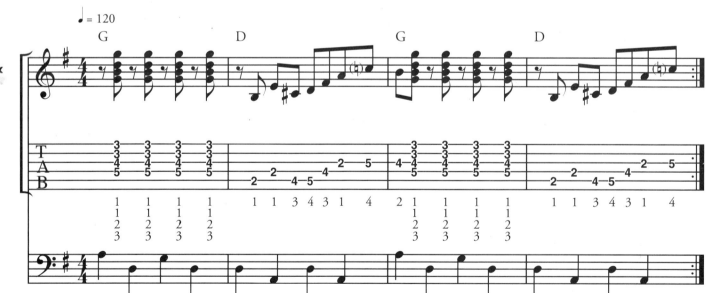

86
Track 96

Below is a tejano accompaniment part where the entire accompaniment is a single-note arpeggio structure played in the classic tejano rhythmic style. This example is the traditional guitar accompaniment to "La Bamba."

Tejano Solo

On the next page is an example with both of the mariachi patterns plus a single-note improvisation over the top of them. The improvisation starts with a *tremolo* picking technique on the note D. Tremolo picking, indicated with the symbol ⚡, is a technique where a note is played repeatedly using alternate picking. The idea is to play as fast as possible creating a loud, sustained sound. Tremolo picking is common to the tejano style. The amplified guitar made it easier for it to cut through and stand out as a single-line solo instrument. The fifth note of the home scale (the note D in the key of G Major) is the central pivot point in the first half of the solo. The second half goes to double stops mostly in 3rds. The double stops are taken from the G Major scale. Notice how the improv doesn't clash with the alternating single-note accompaniment.

Track 98 *Tejano Solo*

Conclusion

Congratulations! You made it to the end of *The Total Latin Guitarist*. We hope you enjoyed studying and playing all of the different Latin styles. As you can see, there is a lot to learn. We hope you use this book as a springboard for further study and discovery. Listen to as much Latin music as you can, and play with musicians who are well-versed in Latin styles. There is so much you can learn just by listening and playing. Good luck!

Appendix

Reading Tablature (TAB)

Tablature, or TAB, is a system used for guitar and other fretted instruments. There are six lines that represent the strings. Numbers are placed on the lines; these numbers tell you what frets to play. Numbers under the TAB staff tell you which left-hand fingers to use. The top line represents the 1st string and the bottom line represents the 6th string. In this book, TAB is written below the corresponding standard music notation.

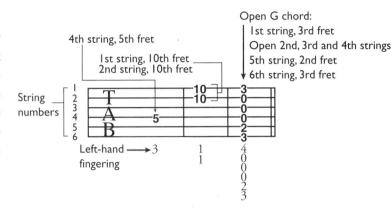

Scale Diagrams

Scale diagrams are horizontal representations of the guitar fretboard that are used to display scale fingerings.

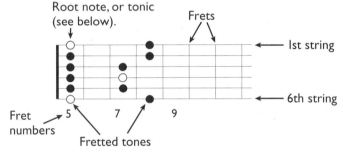

Major Scale Theory

Understanding the *major scale* opens the door to understanding a lot of other music theory. This scale consists of seven notes that proceed in a particular pattern of *whole steps* (two frets) and *half steps* (one fret). The pattern is: whole–whole–half–whole–whole–whole–half.

Each note in the scale is given a number (1–2–3–4–5–6–7) known as a scale *degree*. The 1st scale degree is the *tonic*; this is the note upon which the scale is built and from which it gets its name. Following is a C Major scale.

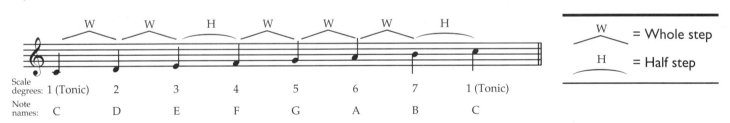

Intervals

An *interval* is the distance between two notes. A whole step and half step are two examples of intervals. In relation to the tonic, any note in the major scale can be considered an interval. Scale degree 2 can be referred to as a 2nd, scale degree 3 as a 3rd, etc.

Note: Any scale degree or interval can be altered with a sharp or flat (♯4, ♭3, etc.). So, referring to the C Major scale above, the 3 (or 3rd) is E, while a ♭3 (or ♭3rd) would be an E♭.

Diatonic Harmony

Diatonic means belonging to a scale or key. Diatonic chords are chords that belong to a particular key. The chords of a major key are built on each tone of the major scale. By stacking *3rds* on top of each scale degree, we get the diatonic chords in the key of C.

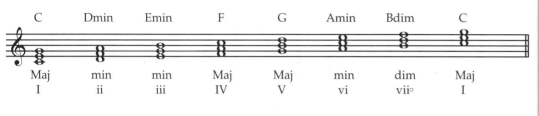

C	Dmin	Emin	F	G	Amin	Bdim	C
Maj	min	min	Maj	Maj	min	dim	Maj
I	ii	iii	IV	V	vi	vii°	I

If you stack one more note on top of each of the chords above, you get all of the diatonic seventh chords. They are as follows: I = Maj7 (major 7th), ii = min7 (minor 7th), iii = min7, IV = Maj7, V = 7 (dominant 7th), vi = min7, vii° = min7♭5.

Circle of 4ths/5ths

To the right is the *circle* (or *cycle*) *of 4ths* or the *circle of 5ths*. As you can see, all 12 major keys (or scales) surround the circle. If you move *counter-clockwise*, each key or scale is exactly four major scale degrees higher than the previous key or scale. (For example, moving C–D–E–F, we see F is a 4th above C.) When looked at from this perspective, this tool is called the circle of 4ths. If you move *clockwise* through the circle, each note is five major scale degrees above the previous note (C–D–E–F–G; G is a 5th above C), which is why this tool can be called the circle of 5ths as well. The C Major scale has no sharps or flats—it's pretty easy to memorize. The major scales F through G♭ each have one more flat than the scale before it. In other words, F has one flat, B♭ has two, E♭ has three, and so on until you reach G♭, which has six flats. The major scales G through F♯ each have one more sharp than the scale before it. So G has one sharp, D has two, A has three, and so on until you reach F♯, which has six sharps. The keys highlighted in gray are *enharmonic equivalents,* which means they sound the same but are spelled differently.

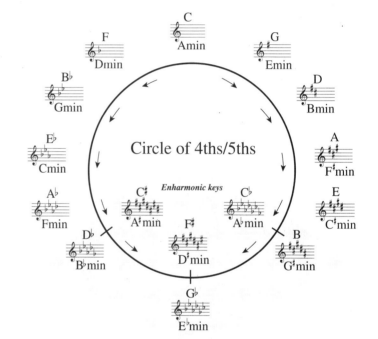

Extended Chords

The term *extended chords* refers to chords that include notes that lie beyond a one-octave major scale. The common tones we add to chords are the 9th, 11th and 13th.

C Major Scale (Two Octaves)

Extended Intervals

9th   11th   13th